15
Highly Effective Instructional Technology Tools

Lynne C. Levy • Frank J. Orlando
Rowan University

KENDALL/HUNT PUBLISHING COMPANY
4050 Westmark Drive   Dubuque, Iowa 52002

Credits

Pgs. 33-34
Courtesy of Ellison Education Equipment.

Pgs. 53-58
Reprinted with permission from *National Educational Technology Standards for Students: Connecting Curriculum and Technology,* © 2002 ISTE ® (International Society for Technology in Education), iste@iste.org, www.iste.org. All rights reserved. Permission does not constitute endorsement by ISTE.

CONTENTS

Preface

The teacher is the key individual in any teaching situation. This is the person who is responsible for planning the sequence of events that will result in the desired student learning. A close look at effective teachers shows that they (1) have well developed and current content area knowledge, (2) demonstrate exceptional planning and organizational skills, (3) are proficient in using a broad array of instructional methods, and (4) are skilled in identifying and using appropriate instructional tools to achieve the desired student learning outcomes. The focus of this book is on the use of instructional tools. It is a practical guide to understanding and using fifteen of the most effective traditional and contemporary instructional technology tools.

When selecting the content for this book, the authors used the definition of "instructional technology" presented in *Instructional Technology: The Definitions and Domains of the Field* by Seels and Richey (Association for Educational Communications and Technology, 1994). In their book, Seels and Richey define Instructional Technology as "the theory and practice of design, development, utilization, management and evaluation of processes and resources for learning." Their four identified sub-categories are: print technologies, audiovisual technologies, computer-based technologies, and integrated technologies.

This book is intended to serve as a primary text for an introductory instructional technology course for teachers; a supplemental text for methods of teaching courses; a handbook for teachers without prior knowledge of these technologies; a resource for teachers wishing to keep current regarding these technologies; a manual for teacher in-service programs; a reference for school librarians; an instructional guide for school media specialists; and a resource for school administrators.

By incorporating these highly effective instructional technology tools we sincerely believe that your success as a teacher will be greatly enhanced. We wish you well.

Lynne C. Levy, Ed.D.
Frank J. Orlando, Ed.D.

Tool

1

Textbooks and Teaching Kits

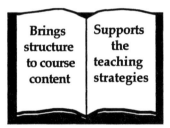

Brings structure to course content

Supports the teaching strategies

1.1 - Introduction

Textbooks are the most common type of instructional print technology used in the educational process. This is because they:
- can be used at a pace that is determined by the student
- can be consulted repeatedly for content clarification and review purposes
- are organized to bring structure to the content area being addressed
- can be made available to all students at a nominal cost
- are easy to use and do not require support technology in order to be used effectively

The selection of a textbook begins with an examination of the course curriculum. This will identify the course content as well as the instructional strategies for teaching the content. Using this data as the initial criteria, information can be secured from publisher's catalogs regarding appropriate materials.

1.2 - Identifying Textbooks and Teaching Kits

In many cases, textbooks are part of a teaching kit available from the publisher. Whereas the textbook has the student as the audience, the supplemental materials in the teaching kit are resources for the teacher. The content of a teaching kit varies, depending on the subject area, grade level and the publisher. Components, all keyed to the student text, may include:

- copy of the student textbook
- an annotated "Teacher's Edition" of the student textbook
- collection of worksheet or activity sheet masters
- transparencies
- quiz and/or test masters
- audio tapes, video tapes, or CDs

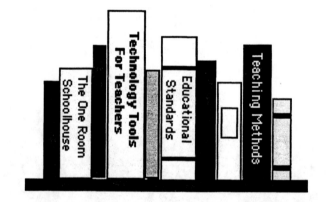

Publisher's Catalogs

The first step in identifying textbooks that are appropriate for a course is to identify publishers that produce materials for the subject area or grade level. This can be done by examining materials that are available in the classroom, talking to other teachers, researching materials that are available in a curriculum library, attending professional conferences, etc. Once the names of publishers have been identified, a copy of the publisher's current catalog or a listing of their current materials must be obtained. This can be done in several ways.

All textbook publishers have a catalog that is available free of charge. Print copies of catalogs are often available for examination in the school library/media center or in the school district's curriculum library. Contact information for most publishers, as well as their current catalog, can usually be found online.

A Copy of the Textbook

After the publisher's catalog (and/or other appropriate literature) has been examined, the next step is to secure a copy of the texts being considered and examine them. In most cases a copy of a text can be requested directly from the publisher. In some cases, however, the publisher will provide the name of the regional representative and requests must be placed with that individual. (Note: Materials will only be sent to teachers and will only be mailed to a school address. Texts will not be sent to pre-service teachers.)

When a copy of the requested textbook is sent, it will be identified as being in one of four categories:

- Complimentary copy   - the book is yours to keep, free of charge.
- Examination copy (free)   - the book is yours to keep, free of charge.
- Examination copy (timed) - the book is yours to review for a period of time (usually 30 to 60 days), after which you must either return the book or pay the specified amount.
- Desk copy   - the book is yours to keep, free of charge, providing you order a specified number of books (usually 10 or more) for your class.

At times, the publisher will provide the entire teaching kit to the teacher. This often entails a preliminary face-to-face meeting with the publisher's representative.

1.3 - Preliminary Evaluation of a Textbook

Every textbook evaluation should begin with a "preliminary evaluation." This 20 to 30 minute procedure will allow the teacher to eliminate texts that obviously are not appropriate for the identified situation. Once the preliminary evaluation has taken place, the remaining texts should be examined using a set of detailed evaluation criteria and a related form. Remember, the evaluation procedure can terminate at any point in the process.

How to Do a Preliminary Evaluation of a Textbook

There are nine steps in the preliminary evaluation of a textbook. In many cases you will eliminate between 50 and 70 percent of the texts from consideration after completing this process.

Step 1 - Identify the copyright date for the text

The copyright date for the text is located on the reverse side of the title page. It will appear in one of the following formats:

- © 2005   • Copyright 2005
- © 2001, 2006   • Copyright 2002, 2005

This is the date when the book was registered with the United States Copyright Office. The content of the text was most likely completed during the previous year or earlier. In some areas (health, geography, science, current events, etc.) the currency of the material is critical to the selection of the text. In other areas (classical literature, basic mathematics, etc.) the copyright date is less critical.

Step 2 - Identify the printing number for the volume you are examining

The printing number for a book is also located on the reverse side of the title page. Usually it will appear near the copyright date. The printing number is a good indication of sales for the text. Printing information appears in one of the following formats:

1 2 3 4 5 6 7 8 9	- numbers in ascending order
9 8 7 6 5 4 3 2 1	- numbers in descending order
1 3 5 7 9 8 6 4 2	- numbers in flip-flop order
a b c d e f g h i	- letters in ascending order
i h g f e d c b a	- letters in descending order
a c e g i h f d b	- letters in flip-flop order

When a printing is sold out and more of the same book are printed, the lowest number or letter is removed from the list:

3 4 5 6 7 8 9	- the book is from the third printing
c e g i h f d b	- the book is from the second printing

Step 3 - Read the preface of the book

If the preface of the book is done following standard practice, it will identify the author's intentions and purpose when writing the book. It will also provide insight into any unique characteristics that have been incorporated into the presentation and identify the underlying philosophy, school of thought, or model the author used.

Step 4 - Read the introduction to the book

If the introduction of the book is done following standard practice, it will provide a brief overview of the content of the text. Major sections should be identified, with key elements for each discussed. A well written introduction is a book review that is biased in favor of the author. It will stress the high points of the text. (Note: Some books will not include a preface and an introduction, but rather will include only one of these two. In many of these cases, the content for both areas has been combined.)

Step 5 - Examine the table of contents

Examine the entire table of contents. It will quickly provide insight into the organization of the materials and the depth and scope of coverage. The primary concern is whether the scope and depth of coverage in the text aligns with the scope and depth of your course of study.

Step 6 - Visually examine every page of the book

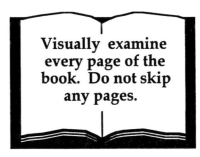

Beginning with the title page and ending with the last page of the index of the book, visually examine every page of the text. Do not skip any pages. This examination can be done as quickly as you can turn the pages. You are not reading, you are imprinting layout design and special features of the book in your mind. You are acquiring a "sense of the text." After completing this process you will have an understanding of the length of the chapters or units and knowledge regarding the use of illustrations, diagrams, and charts; whether key words are in bold type; if concepts are identified throughout the reading; etc.

Step 7 - Read any three to five pages for readability appropriateness

Select any three to five pages of text and read them from the perspective of your students. Your primary concern is whether they will be able to read and comprehend the writing, the presentation, and the organizational style.

Step 8 - Select a topic and read any three to five pages for content

Select a topic from the Table of Contents in which you are well-versed regarding the current state of the research. Select and read any three to five pages from that section of the text. The purpose is to determine the clarity of presentation, currency of content, and accuracy of the material.

Step 9 - Select texts for closer examination

After completing this preliminary evaluation you should be able to eliminate books that clearly do not meet your instructional needs. Use the evaluation criteria in the following section to undertake a more extensive evaluation of the remaining texts.

1.4 - Detailed Evaluation of a Textbook

A number of factors should be considered when doing a detailed evaluation a textbook. Although all of them may not be appropriate in every instance, each will be discussed and each is included in the sample "Textbook Evaluation Form" that appears in this chapter.

How to Critically Evaluate a Textbook

After doing a preliminary evaluation of the various textbooks being considered, use the following evaluation criteria to select texts and support materials that are best suited to your specific teaching situation.

- **Author Qualifications**
  Is the author knowledgeable in the content area? Does the author have practical experience on the level addressed in the textbook?

- **Relevance to Course Curriculum**
  Does the overall content of the textbook correlate with your identified course curriculum?

- **Scope and Depth of Coverage**
  Is the scope and depth consistent with the scope and depth prescribed in your course outline?

- **Objective Presentation of Content**
  Is the content presented in an objective manner and free of bias? Is there a balance of presentation when two opposing points of view are discussed?

- **Currentness of Content**
  Is the material in the textbook current? Do any components "date" the book?

- **Logical Organization**
  Is the textbook organized in a manner that is logical and easy for the students to understand?

- **Clear Writing**
  Is the writing clear and understandable? Is the author's "outline" easily discernible by the reader?

- **Appropriate Reading Level**
  Is the textbook written at a reading level that is appropriate for the class and the students? Is the textbook adaptable for students at differing reading levels?

- **Identified Measurable Objectives**
  Have objectives for each unit or chapter been identified? Are they measurable?

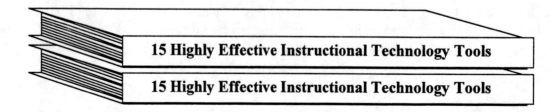

15 Highly Effective Instructional Technology Tools

15 Highly Effective Instructional Technology Tools

- **Vocabulary Words**
  Are new words and terms highlighted or given special attention in the section where they are introduced? Are the definitions clear and easy to understand?

- **Review Questions**
  Are review questions identified for each unit or chapter of the textbook? Is there a mix of questions that are directly based on the textbook? Are they open-ended?

- **References and Resources**
  Are references for the content of the textbook included? Are additional resources identified for the reader that wishes to investigate the topic more extensively?

- **Illustrations**
  Are illustrations in black-and-white or color? Are they used throughout the text? Are they dated due to clothing, styles, etc.? Do they show individuals similar to the readers of the textbook in terms of age, grade, etc.?

- **Diagrams, Charts, and Drawings**
  Are they in black-and-white or color? Are they used throughout the textbook? Do they clarify the content being discussed? Is there variety in style and use?

- **Overall Layout**
  Is the textbook interesting? Does it draw the reader into its pages? Is there a balance of text, illustrations, charts, diagrams, etc. throughout the textbook?

- **Diversity**
  Does the textbook have a multicultural presentation? Does it include physically and mentally challenged individuals in the discussion of content and the use of examples?

- **Binding**
  Is the type of binding appropriate for the intended use of the textbook? Are various types of bindings available?

- **Cost**
  Is the cost of the textbook inline with other books of a similar type? Is the cost within the budget available?

- **Support Materials**
  Are there support materials such as teacher guides, workbooks, test banks, etc., available?

- **Other Considerations**
  What other factors must be considered due to the uniqueness of your situation?

1.5 - Textbook Evaluation Form

The following example of a textbook evaluation form is based on the content in this chapter. After a preliminary evaluation has been completed, a form such as this will provide a uniform set of criteria for doing a critical evaluation of a textbook. The form would be used to evaluate two or more textbooks and make comparisons that will result in a more valid decision when selecting a textbook.

TEXTBOOK EVALUATION FORM

Part I – Course Information

Course: _____ Grade(s): _____

Brief Description of Course: _____

_____

Part II – Textbook Information

Book One:

Title: _____

Author(s): _____

Publisher: _____

Copyright Date: _____ Edition: _____ No. of Pages: _____

Book Two:

Title: _____

Author(s): _____

Publisher: _____

Copyright Date: _____ Edition: _____ No. of Pages: _____

Part III – Critical Evaluations

Directions: Using the rating system identified below, evaluate each of the selected textbooks. It is important that you are consistent in your interpretation and application of the criteria.

Check the appropriate box for each item:

5 = Excellent   2 = Below Average
4 = Above Average   1 = Poor
3 = Average   0 = Does Not Apply

	Book One						Book Two					
	5	4	3	2	1	0	5	4	3	2	1	0
Author Qualifications												
Relevance to Course Curriculum												
Scope of Coverage												
Depth of Coverage												
Objective Presentation of Content												
Currentness of Content												
Logical Organization												
Clear Writing												
Appropriate Reading Level												
Identified Measurable Objectives												
Identified Vocabulary Terms												
Identified Review Questions												
Identified References/Resources												
Illustrations - Black & White												
Illustrations - Color												
Diagrams, Charts, Drawings - Black & White												
Diagrams, Charts, Drawings - Color												
Overall Layout												
Text/Illustrations - Multicultural												
Text/Illustrations - Disabled Individuals												
Appropriate Binding												
Appropriate Cost												
Support Materials - Teacher's Edition of Text												
Support Materials - Teacher's Guide/Manual												
Support Materials - Workbooks												
Support Materials - Assessment Materials												
Support Materials - Media/Technology												

Total Score Awarded: _____   _____

1.6 - Activities

• Activity One •

Identify the names of three educational publishers. Select a grade level (K-12) and a subject area (e.g. math, science, language arts) and go to the Web sites for the three publishers. (Use *Google* to identify the Web address.) Select one textbook from each publisher's online catalog and compare the information provided and the materials available. Based on this information, write a two-page (word processed, double-spaced) report comparing and contrasting the three texts.

• Activity Two •

Go to a curriculum resource center or an instructional resource center and select a teaching kit for examination. The kit must include--at minimum--the student textbook, the teacher's edition of the textbook, and an activity book or workbook. Examine the various items of the kit and write a two-page (word processed, double-spaced) review of the teaching kit. Discuss the advantages and disadvantages of the components.

• Activity Three •

Select two teaching kits that address the same subject and grade level (grades K-12). Make a copy of the "Textbook Evaluation Form" in section 1.5 and do a comparative evaluation of the two student textbooks and their supporting materials.

Instructional Boards

2.1 - Introduction

"Instructional boards" is the name given to the broad array of boards or surfaces that are used to provide information during the process of instruction. The most common types of instructional boards are chalkboards, multipurpose boards (also called white boards or marker boards), and bulletin boards. All of these items provide the user with a means of providing information to the class. They also afford the opportunity to easily change the information at any time.

2.2 - Chalkboards

Chalkboards have a long and noble history in the educational tools arena. Traditionally, white chalk was used to write on slate boards called blackboards. Today, chalk and chalkboards are both available in a variety of colors. Despite the fact that this technology has changed little over the years, the chalkboard is still a valuable instructional technology tool for the teacher.

Non-Magnetic Chalkboards

Contemporary, non-magnetic chalkboards consist of a writing surface on a backing of a material that is not magnetic (Masonite, composition board, etc.). These boards are the least costly to purchase.

AaBbCcDdEeFfGgHhIiJjKkLlMmNnOoPpQqRrSsTtUuVvWwXxYyZz

White Chalk is the primary color of chalk used on a black chalkboard.

Yellow chalk is the primary color of chalk used on a green chalkboard.

Magnetic Chalkboards

Many educational settings have chalkboards that are a combination chalk/magnetic board. Unlike the less costly chalkboards, these boards are designed to withstand extensive and long-term use. Since they have a base surface of metal (usually porcelain on steel) they will accept magnetic accessories. This allows the teacher to display posters, charts, maps, student work, etc. on the board without the worry of damaging the writing surface. The materials used in this situation can also be easily and quickly displayed, used, and removed.

2.3 - Multipurpose Boards

Multipurpose boards are also known as "white boards" or "marker boards." The name white board is based on the fact that the writing surface is white. The marker board name emerged from the use of dry erase markers as the writing instrument used on the board surface.

The name "multipurpose board" is more accurate because the board can be used for a variety of purposes. It can be written on using dry erase markers (no other type should be used); it can serve as a projection screen for any projection technology (overhead, slide, video, etc.); shapes cut from thin plastic sheets will adhere to the surface if rubbed in place; and those with a steel back can be used as a magnetic display board for posters, student work, etc. Using a split screen approach, any combination of these options is also possible.

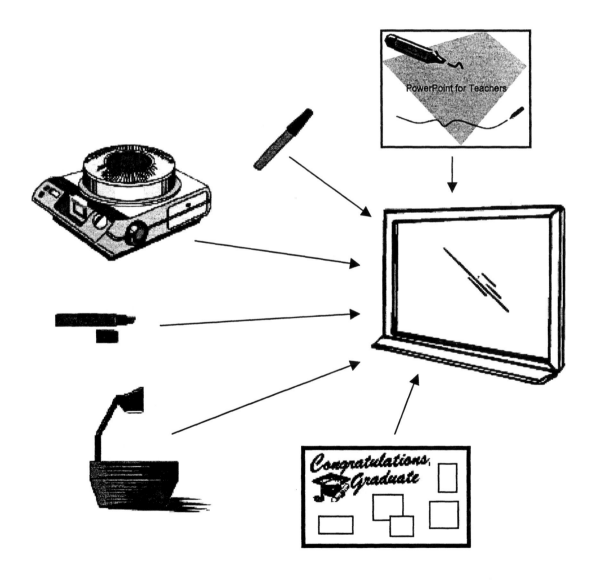

2.4 - Bulletin Boards

Bulletin boards are the most common form of display technology used in the classroom. Although they are intended to provide information or an opportunity for interaction to a large number of students they can also serve as a link and point of unification for special interest groups.

All bulletin boards can be grouped into one of three categories: decorative, motivational, and instructional.

> • **Decorative Bulletin Boards**
>   - used to help create a visually stimulating educational environment.
>
> • **Motivational Bulletin Boards**
>   - inspire students to reach further in their quest for learning or to take action.
>
> • **Instructional Bulletin Boards**
>   - tied to specific curricular objectives and provide instruction.

Motivational bulletin boards and instructional bulletin boards are the two primary categories that all teachers should become proficient in creating and using in their teaching. Bulletin boards in these categories can be either "static" (traditional) or "interactive."

> • **Static Bulletin Boards**
>   - present information.
>
> • **Interactive Bulletin Boards**
>   - require student activity.

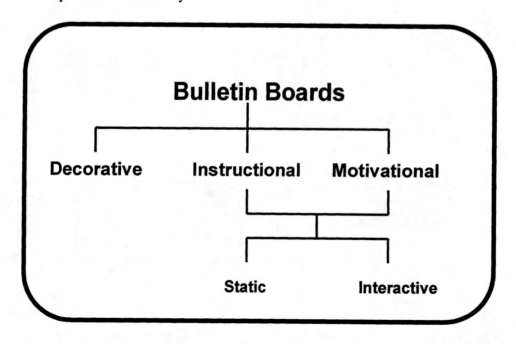

How To Develop A Bulletin Board

Although many books describe the development of bulletin boards, there are six basic steps involved in the process:

1. **Identify the subject and theme**
   Identify this with as much specificity as possible. This will greatly facilitate the remaining steps. Planning at this point will reduce the number of questions that may arise later in the process.

2. **Identify your primary objective(s)**
   What do you want to take place? How? When? Your objective(s) should be clearly stated so that the student has the same understanding of the expectations from the bulletin board as the teacher.

3. **Develop a working layout or plan**
   Brainstorm ideas. Determine if the bulletin board will be static or interactive. Make "thumbnail" sketches of various layouts. Put them aside for a day. Evaluate them again. Needed changes will be more readily evident. Ask another person to look at your plans. Revise. Then, make a detailed plan of your final layout.

4. **Acquire or create the materials needed**
   Gather and/or create the materials necessary for the final layout. Lead time is usually required in order to create an effective bulletin board. The voids that are evident in hastily developed bulletin boards are easy to spot.

5. **Put up the bulletin board**
   When the bulletin board is in place, inform the class regarding its purpose and relationship to the content area under study. Tell the students what is expected of them. Discuss their use of the bulletin board.

6. **Evaluate the success of the bulletin board**
   Evaluate the bulletin board from your perspective as a teacher. Have the students evaluate the success of the bulletin board. (Develop a simple form that asks about content, clarity, interest, etc.)

After the bulletin board has been taken down, save the individual components either for reassembly at another time or for reuse in other bulletin boards. Write down and save your evaluation of the current bulletin board. It will be useful in future planning for other bulletin boards and classes.

Static (Traditional) Bulletin Boards

Static (traditional) bulletin boards present information without requiring the student to directly respond to the information.

They can be used as an introduction to a topic, a review of the content covered, enrichment regarding a class topic, a means to elicit action from the reader, etc.

Interactive Bulletin Boards

Interactive bulletin boards require the student to engage in some type of activity that is directly tied to the content and materials on the bulletin board. The expected actions are necessary in order to fully benefit from the design of the bulletin board. Like a static bulletin board, the focus could be to introduce or summarize a topic, provide enrichment, etc.

Activity Sheets

Interactive bulletin boards also have one other unique characteristic. An activity sheet accompanies the bulletin board.

Activity sheets identify questions the student must answer and activities that may, or must be, undertaken. Answers to complete some of the activities are found on the bulletin board. Others must be found elsewhere (textbook, almanac, encyclopedia, atlas, internet, etc.).

An activity sheet for an interactive bulletin board on New Jersey might contain the following questions that could be answered using the bulletin board: *What city is the capital of New Jersey? Who is the current governor? Identify two inventors from New Jersey. Name two major companies that are based in New Jersey.* Questions that would require using other sources could be: *Who was the governor of New Jersey in 1950? Identify the bibliographic information for a biography of a New Jersey inventor. Identify a Web site that discusses recreational areas in New Jersey.*

Guidelines To Effective Bulletin Board Design

- ### The "Rule of Thirds"

  Divide your layout area like a tic-tac-toe board. The "rule of thirds" states that the four points of line intersection are good areas to place key elements in your layout.

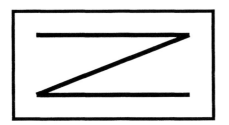

- ### The Reading "Z"

  The reading "Z" principle states that most people read across the top of a page, then diagonally down to the bottom, and finally across the bottom.

- ### The "Upper Third" Rule

  This rule states that the upper third of the layout area is the most powerful place for the title and other key elements.

15 Hints For Successful Bulletin Boards

1. **Use one idea or concept for your theme**
   Keep it simple and to the point. When there are many trees in the forest, it's easy to get lost.

2. **Identify one primary objective and stay focused**
   Everything should relate to meeting your identified objective. It is your focal point.

3. **Plan and re-plan on paper, not on the board**
   Identify what you will need to meet your objective and determine how it will be done.

4. **Do not restrict yourself to the materials at hand**
   Find and/or create the needed materials. This should not be a collage of the materials that are available in the classroom.

5. **Follow the rules for lettering and headings**
   Headline lettering should be readable from across the room. The title should draw students near.

6. **Try various layout plans**
   Start with the assumption that you must identify three possible layouts.

7. **Use a layout that is dynamic and visually appealing**
   Take a hint from billboards and ads in popular magazines. Excitement and education do mix.

8. **Make effective use of color**
   Use color to attract attention, show differences, and emphasize content.

9. **Incorporate balance (formal or informal) and unity**
   Use a variety of layout designs in bulletin boards. Examine advertisements for examples.

10. **Capture the viewer's interest and hold it**
    Use the layout, colors, and topic to generate interest. Content should follow through on it.

11. **Identify follow-up or related activities**
    Build on the interest generated by the bulletin board by having required and/or optional activities.

12. **Don't overload the layout or design**
    Too much of any element can be confusing and undermine the layout.

13. **Address issues that are timely and interesting**
    Build on student interests and concerns by addressing them in a bulletin board.

14. **Talk to the class about the bulletin board**
    Teacher/student discussion is essential if you are to get the full value from a bulletin board.

15. **Take the bulletin board down in a timely fashion**
    Once the bulletin board has served its purpose, replace it.

Ideas For Content Area Bulletin Boards

Social Studies	• State History • Current Events	• Map Skills • Government
Language Arts	• Poetry • Famous Writers	• Science Fiction • Types of Writing
Science	• Solar Energy • Electricity	• Plants • Recycling
Math	• Metric System • Geometric Design	• Graphs • Calculators
Health	• Foods • AIDS	• Personal Hygiene • Family Planning
Art	• Art Deco • Famous Painters	• Cartoonists • Art Museums
Music	• Famous Composers • Instruments	• Rap Music • ASCAP
Vocational Education	• Technical Careers • Apprenticeship	• Unions • Tools of the Trade
Physical Education	• Famous Athletes • Evolution of Games	• Rules and Regulations • Baseball
Safety	• OSHA • First Aid	• Rules of the Road • Bicycle Safety

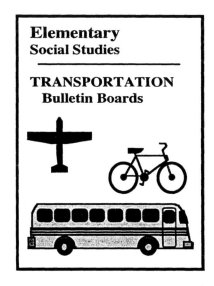

Elementary
Social Studies

TRANSPORTATION
Bulletin Boards

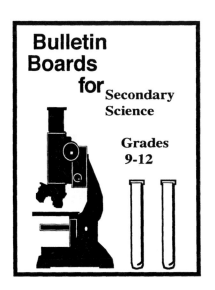

Bulletin Boards for Secondary Science

Grades 9-12

2.5 - Activities

• Activity One •

Design a static instructional bulletin board that relates to a lesson or unit you will be or could be teaching. Start by creating three preliminary layouts. Select the best idea and develop it on a large piece of paper. Identify the grade level, course, unit topic, lesson topic, and the bulletin board objective(s) on the back of the paper.

• Activity Two •

Design an interactive instructional bulletin board and the related activity sheet. Sketch the layout of the bulletin board, develop an activity sheet that has a minimum of 10 questions, and prepare an answer sheet for the activity sheet questions. Identify the grade level, course, unit topic, lesson topic, and the bulletin board objective(s).

• Activity Three •

Design a motivational bulletin board intended to solicit donations of canned goods for the victims of a natural disaster.

Tool

3

Learning Centers
and
Learning Stations

3.1 - Introduction

The constructivist classroom has received considerable attention in recent years. Far removed from the rote memorization approach to learning, constructivism is concerned with students learning "how to learn." Constructivists believe that knowledge acquisition and learning result from hands-on experiences. The student "constructs" an understanding of concepts and a knowledge base as a result of his/her interactions in the real world.

Classrooms that support a constructivist approach to learning are places where individual, collaborative, and competitive activities are commonplace. One of the major questions for constructivists is "How can I provide meaningful educational experiences for a variety of interests, in many areas, on different levels?" The use of learning centers and learning stations is a viable answer to this question.

3.2 - Learning Centers and Learning Stations

One of the first questions asked by anyone researching this topic deals with the use of the phrases "learning center" and "learning station." Is a learning center the same as a learning station? And if not, what is the difference? Articles can be found that will take either side of this issue and defend that stand. The majority of the research does view a learning center as different from a learning station.

Generally, a learning center deals with a broad area of knowledge or study. There can be learning centers dealing with mathematics, science, social studies, art, physical education, music, etc. However, learning centers could also deal with areas such as the state of New Jersey, the Civil War, space exploration, etc.

Learning stations are usually narrow in scope and are frequently found as subdivisions of a learning center. Although learning stations are often smaller than learning centers, that is not always the case. In some instances a learning station can be as extensive in scope and size as a learning center. As a general rule, the guidelines for a creating a learning center can be directly applied to a learning station.

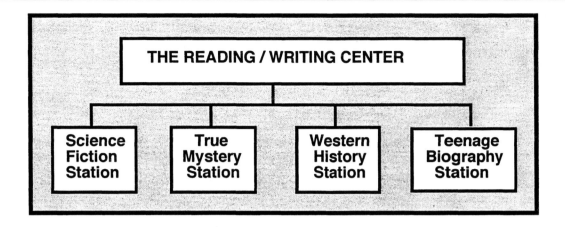

3.3 - Five Basic Questions Regarding Learning Centers

There are five basic questions that must be answered before the teacher can plan, create, and implement a learning center (Note: When the phrase "learning center" is used in this chapter it will mean "learning center" or "learning station.")

1. What is a learning center?
2. What are the major characteristics of a learning center?
3. What types of materials are found at a learning center?
4. What does a learning center look like?
5. How is the work or progress of the student assessed?

What is a learning center?

A learning center is a self-contained learning environment where one student, or a small group of students, can independently investigate an area of study in order to meet a predetermined objective. The center includes all the materials, supplies, equipment, and directions needed to undertake a series of activities.

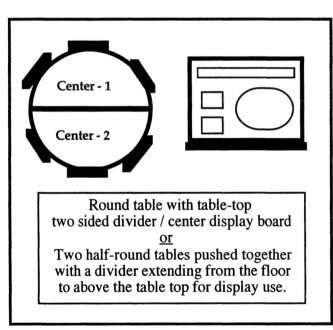

Round table with table-top
two sided divider / center display board
or
Two half-round tables pushed together
with a divider extending from the floor
to above the table top for display use.

A table with file cabinets on
either side is ideal for a
quiet learning center.

23

What are the major characteristics of a learning center?

All learning centers have:

- A clear label or title
- Sequenced activities
- Optional activities
- All needed supplies
- Information resources

- Identified objectives
- Basic/required activities
- All needed materials
- All needed equipment
- Directions for activities

Directions for learning center activities can be presented in a variety of ways: video tapes, audiotapes, instructional notebooks, photograph series, task cards, etc. Task cards can be made using 5" x 8" index cards. They can be laminated and/or held together with a notebook ring.

Learning centers are:

- Structured for individual or small group participation - determined by the teacher.
- Self-instructing - the teacher is not needed for successful center use.
- Self-correcting - the student has immediate feedback regarding success in undertaking or completing an activity.
- Paced by the student - starting and stopping is at the discretion of the student.
- Designed for different purposes - they can introduce, develop, or reinforce a concept; foster enrichment; develop awareness; create interest; etc.

What types of materials are found at a learning center?

Learning centers may include:

- Textbooks and resource books
- Teaching kits
- A concept map
- Manipulatives to undertake the activities
- Support materials (paper, scissors, tape, card stock, etc.)
- Photographs of other students engaged in the activity
- Directions in multiple formats (task cards, a video, etc.)
- Technology to instruct (VCR, audio cassette player, videodiscs/player, slide viewer)
- Technology to record results (camcorder, camera, tapes)
- Computer
- Internet connection
- Individual logs or record sheets/folders
- Examples of previous student work
- Lists of selected Web sites
- Lists of resource/reference books in the school library

What does a learning center look like?

The structure, location, and appearance of a learning center is determined on a case-by-case basis. The examples in this chapter are representative of commonly found learning center designs. Tables and desks are the natural starting point for creating a learning center.

Four desks pushed together with a two-sided divider / center display board.

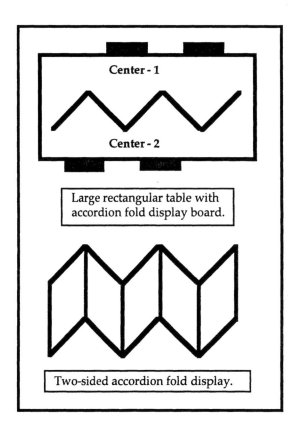

Large rectangular table with accordion fold display board.

Two-sided accordion fold display.

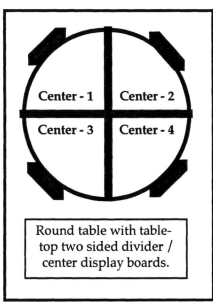

Round table with table-top two sided divider / center display boards.

Table-top display board.

How is the work or progress of the student assessed?

Student progress at a learning center is assessed on two fronts: by the student and by the teacher.

Self-assessment by the student should be completed at the end of each and every work period at the center. This can be done in a number of ways. The student could:

- keep a journal of his/her center activity
- record activity in individual logs or folders at the center
- keep an audio record of the activity
- keep a photographic record of results
- maintain a portfolio

Assessment by the teacher is a periodic process. This can be done by:

- reviewing student logs or journals
- listening to audiotape reports
- viewing photographic or video tape records
- meeting with students individually to review progress
- reviewing individual portfolios
- keeping an ongoing photographic record of student activity

3.4 - How to Plan, Create, and Implement a Learning Center

Planning and preparation are the key components to effective lessons. They are also the keys to successfully using learning centers as an educational tool. The following steps are essential to the process:

1. identify the center area, topic, or concept
2. identify the center title
3. identify the center objective(s)
4. identify the basic activity
5. identify the optional activities
6. determine a physical location
7. develop a concept map/web showing the place of the center in the larger area of study
8. design the center layout
9. design and create a display board
10. identify and assemble/create the materials and supplies required to do the basic and optional activities
11. gather the equipment/technology required to do the basic and optional activities
12. develop an instructional package (task cards, video tapes, activity flow charts, etc.) that will guide the student through the successful completion of the activities
13. gather the support resource materials

14. develop a system to record individual student activity at the center (log, journal, report folders, etc.)
15. set up the center to be visually appealing
16. do a "dry run" of all the activities using only the directions, materials, supplies, and equipment provided
17. revise the directions and add needed materials to assure correct completion of the activities
18. develop a plan for infusing the center into the instructional schedule
19. introduce the center to the class with a brief presentation

3.5 - Evaluating a Learning Center

One of the most valuable activities that a teacher can undertake regarding a learning center is to have other teachers and/or users of the center complete an evaluation form. This will not only provide input when restructuring the center the next time it is used; it will provide valuable insight when you undertake the development of additional learning centers, as well. What follows is an example of a learning center evaluation form. Note that the name of the evaluator is not part of the form.

Learning Center Evaluation Form

Center Name_____

Overall Visual Appeal; Setup	5	4	3	2	1
Title and Objective(s)	5	4	3	2	1
Basic Activity; Directions	5	4	3	2	1
Optional Activity; Directions	5	4	3	2	1
Grade Level: Appropriate, Value	5	4	3	2	1
Materials, Supplies, Equipment	5	4	3	2	1
Procedure to Record Progress	5	4	3	2	1

What is the most appealing element of this learning center?

What is the weakest element of this learning center?

What one suggestion would you make that would improve the effectiveness of this learning center?

Additional Comments:

3.6 - Activities

• Activity One •

Identify a broad topic for a learning center and discuss the purpose and objectives the learning center will address. Name and describe three learning stations that could be part of this center. For each of the stations, identify your objectives, the basic activities, and the optional activities.

• Activity Two •

On a large sheet of paper, draw the layout of a learning center for a topic of your choice. On the back of the paper identify the center name, objectives, and grade level. Briefly describe two basic activities and two optional activities for this center. The layout on the front of the paper must reflect the material identified on the back of the paper.

• Activity Three •

Plan and create a learning center for a lesson or unit you will be teaching. Test the center by having two students use the center as intended. Watch the students as they undertake the activities. Make note of any problems that occur during this test phase. Have each student evaluate the center. Redesign the center using your notes and the student evaluations.

Tool
4

Lettering Machines
and
Die-Cut Letters

4.1 - Introduction

Lettering is an important element in virtually every teacher-made instructional aid used in the classroom. Posters, bulletin boards, handouts, learning centers, and transparencies all rely on lettering to help convey the intended message. If the letters are too small, difficult to read, or amateurish in their presentation, the instructional aid will fail to fulfill its intended purpose.

Lettering techniques can generally be grouped under one of four primary categories: (1) handmade letters, (2) ready-made letters, (3) mechanical letters, and (4) computer generated letters. Regardless of what technique is used to produce the letters, there are some basic rules that apply to all situations.

In the first part of this chapter we will discuss lettering guidelines that apply to the development of all instructional aids that incorporate the use of lettering. The second part of the chapter will concentrate on die-cut letters, with emphasis on the family of *Ellison®* lettering machines and tools.

4.2 - Lettering Guidelines

Guidelines for effective lettering deal with letter size, letter style, and the spacing between letters and words. Letters must be of a sufficient size and style to allow for easy reading. Each element contributes to an effective and readable product.

Lettering Styles

When selecting a letter style, often called a face or a font, the rule is "simple is better." Sans-serif (without the end stroke) letters and gothic letters are bolder and easier to read than letter styles that have a serif or ornamental style.

This is Century Gothic in 12 point, 14 point, **24 point**

This is Chicago in 12 point, 14 point, **24 point**

This is Helvetica in 12 point, 14 point, **24 point**

This is Librarian in 12 point, 14 point, 24 point

This is New York in 12 point, 14 point, 24 point

This is Times New Roman in 12 point, 14 point, 24 point

This is Signboard in 12 point, 14 point, **24 point**

Additional options include selecting plain, outline, shadow, or italic lettering formats.

This is Geneva font, Plain lettering, 14 point.

This is Geneva font, Outline lettering, 14 point.

This is Geneva font, Heading 1 lettering, 14 point.

This Is Geneva font, Italic lettering, 14 point.

For short titles, use all capital letters. If four or more words are used in the title, it is better to use lowercase letters with capital letters used for the first letter in the primary words.

• AMERICA •

GEORGE WASHINGTON

America: Yesterday, Today, and Tomorrow

When longer headings or entire sentences are a part of the display, serif (with the end stroke) letters should be used. They are more readable when longer text is involved.

The Civil Rights Movement in America: A History

Lettering Techniques

Posters, bulletin boards, displays, and learning stations all depend upon letters to identify their theme and present content to the student. These letters can be produced using a variety of techniques that can be grouped into four categories. The primary methods for each category are discussed here.

Handmade Letters

Handmade letters can be made using a marking instrument (pen, crayon, marker, brush), or they can be cut out of a variety of different materials using scissors.

- **Felt pen lettering** is usually done directly on the surface where the letters will be used. Markers are available in two types: permanent ink and water-based ink. Permanent ink markers are used to either draw the entire letter or draw the outline of a letter. When the outline only is drawn, the letter can be filled in with color using a water-based marker.

- **Cut-out letters** can be made in one of two ways. They can be traced from a template or the letter can be projected onto the selected material using an overhead projector and traced. The letters are then cut out with scissors.

Ready-Made Letters

Ready-made letters require little or no preparation in order to use them. Examples include precut letters and adhesive-backed letters.

- **Precut letters** are available in a variety of sizes, materials, and styles. They are direct cutouts from a material such as cardboard, paper, felt, plastic, etc. Some have a special backing for mounting (pins, hooks, slots) on a particular type of surface.

- **Adhesive-backed letters** are made from a variety of materials (vinyl, paper, felt). The letters are peeled off of the backing sheet and applied where desired. Although there are many sizes and styles that are easy to use, they are one of the more expensive options for lettering.

Mechanical Letters

There are many mechanical lettering systems in use, but the two that are most frequently used in the preparation of posters, bulletin boards, and learning stations are stencils and die-cut letters.

- **Stencils** are commonly used in the elementary classroom. They are available in many sizes and are usually made of heavy paper, plastic, or metal. The stencil is used to outline the letter on the desired surface. Then the letter is completed with markers, crayons, paint, etc.

- **Die-cut letters** are made using a metal cutter mounted in a wooden holder. These are discussed in the next section of this chapter.

Computer-Generated Letters

All word processing programs will allow the user to generate letters, words, and titles using various type styles (faces or fonts) and in almost any size desired. In addition, software packages that have special features to create banners and posters are available.

4.3 - Die-Cut Letters

Die-cut letters and shapes can be used for signs, bulletin boards, posters, and many other educational projects. They are made using a die that consists of a metal cutter that is mounted in a wooden holder. The material is cut using the die, producing perfect letters, numbers, or shapes every time.

For more than 25 years, the most popular letter and shape die-cutting tools used by educators have been made by *Ellison*. In addition to manufacturing several styles of die-cutting tools, the company has a catalog of nearly 10,000 dies. The content in this section is based on materials produced by *Ellison*.

Dies: Alphabet, Number, and Shape

Dies are available in a variety of sizes. Alphabet and number dies are the starting point for any collection. Shape dies to fit the educational needs of the situation are then chosen to round off the collection.

3" to 8" alphabet and number dies are formatted as "single-up" -- one letter is contained on each die.

1-1/4" and 2" alphabet and number dies are formatted with multiple letters and numbers on each die.

Music			
Fall			
Presidents			
Science			
School			

• **Examples of Shape Dies** •

Materials

The most frequently asked question regarding using die-cutters is: "What materials can I cut using these dies? The answer is simple. If you can cut the material with a regular pair of scissors, you can cut it with a die-cutter. Examples of materials commonly cut with die-cutters include:

- contruction paper
- wall paper
- aluminum foil
- static cling vinyl

- file folders
- shelf paper
- fabric
- card stock

- oak tag
- felt
- poly foam
- greeting cards

How to Make Die-Cut Letters

When cutting out letters or shapes, place the material (paper, card stock, poster board, felt, plastic, wall paper, etc.) under the cutting edge of the die and insert the die and material packet in the hand-powered machine. (Note: The material must be precut to the size of the die, since both the die and the material must be placed in the machine.) When the handle of the machine is lowered, the die cuts the material. When the handle is raised, the die and the die-cut shapes can be removed.

1. Raise the handle all the way up.

2. Place the paper, or other material, against the rubber side of the die.

3. Turn the die over and slide it into the machine, rubber side down.

4. Center the die under the pressure plate of the machine.

5. Bring the handle down to cut through the material.

6. Raise the handle slowly in order to prevent it from springing back and causing injury.

7. Remove the die and the material from the machine.

4.4 - Activities

• Activity One •

Design a bulletin board that incorporates different die-cut letters or shapes. (1) Use large die-cut letters for the title. (2) Use a different style and size letter in the layout of the bulletin board. (3) Incorporate three or more die-cut shapes in the design.

• Activity Two •

Create a poster that uses die-cut letters for the title and incorporates four different die-cut shapes in the layout.

• Activity Three •

Design a display board for a learning center that: (1) Uses die-cut letters for the title. (2) Incorporates three or more shapes in the display board design. (3) Uses the shapes to connect to other materials at the center (e.g. activity book, resource materials, record sheets, etc.).

Tool

5

Overhead Projectors and Transparencies

5.1 - Introduction

The overhead projector is not only very easy to use, but it is also the most common type of projection technology available in schools. Unlike other projection technologies that are "dated" and have   limited current resources available (16mm films and filmstrips) or are costly (video projectors), overhead projectors are available in many models and at affordable prices.

Overhead transparencies are used with an overhead projector. They are one of the most frequently used and popular instructional tools employed by teachers. In addition to being easy to make and use, overhead transparencies offer a number of other advantages to the teacher. They can be interspersed with other forms of technology, they can be customized and manipulated in a number of ways, and the pace is fully controlled by the teacher.

Visual presenters are also used in the classroom for projection. In addition to projecting overhead transparencies, they can also project books and other paper documents, photographs, 35mm slides, and 3-dimenstional objects.

5.2 - Overhead Projectors

The broad appeal of the overhead projector in both the educational community and the business sector is largely tied to its unique advantages as an instruction/presentation tool. Normal classroom lighting can be maintained while using the overhead projector, thus the instructor can have better control of the class.

Moreover, because the projector is placed in the front of the classroom, with projection taking place over the shoulders of the presenter, the instructor is always facing the class. The variety of uses and the control afforded the instructor over the presentation of materials when using the overhead projector is enhanced by its light weight, ease of operation, and reasonable cost.

The basic design consists of a box with a glass platen (called the stage) on the top surface. A powerful lamp is mounted above a reflector on the floor of the box. When the overhead projector is turned on, the light is reflected off the reflector, through a fresnel lens (causing the light to be evenly distributed across the stage), and through the stage. The light continues through the transparency on the stage and the image is transferred to a projection lens and mirror that is mounted above the box. This mechanism turns the image 90 degrees and projects it onto the screen.

The stage area of most overhead projectors is 10" by 10", allowing the user to project images that are this size or smaller. Focus is attained in two ways: (1) moving the overhead projector closer to or further away from the screen and (2) raising or lowering the projection lens using the focus knob.

Using the Overhead Projector

There are many models of overhead projectors available, ranging from the standard tabletop models to the collapsible/portable models. The following procedures apply to most overhead projectors. Prior to using any overhead projector, consult the manufacturer's operator's manual for product-specific directions.

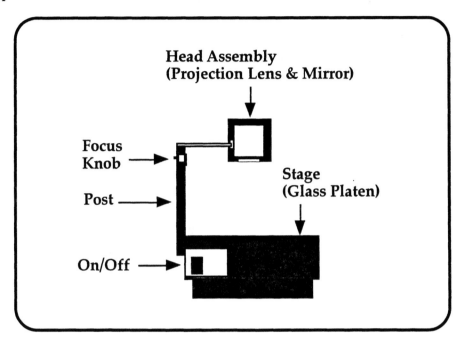

Standard tabletop overhead projectors are generally larger in size than the collapsible/portable models. Although these models do not "fold up," many have a handle to allow for easy transportation from one location to another.

1. Position the projector in front of the screen.
2. Uncoil and plug in the power cord.
3. Turn on the projector.
4. Move the projector and/or tilt the projection lens/mirror so the image space fills the screen without distortion.
5. Place a test transparency on the stage.
6. Focus the image using the focus knob.
7. USE the overhead projector.
8. Turn off the projector.
9. Unplug the power cord and return to storage area.

Collapsible/portable overhead projectors are less cumbersome than the standard tabletop models and are specifically constructed to be portable. To begin using a portable model, the stage door must first be opened. The stage and head assembly are then locked in place. When finished using the projector, the stage cover is opened; the head assembly and post are unlocked and folded in, and the stage cover is closed.

Overhead Projector Lamps

The most common "problem" when using the overhead projector is a burned out lamp (bulb). Most projectors have a spare lamp installed as part of the lamp assembly; others house only a single lamp. If a spare lamp is available, switch to this alternate or second lamp. Procedures vary depending upon the model.

If the lamp is burned out and must be replaced:
1. Unplug the projector.
2. Open the cover or panel to reveal the lamp. (Be sure the lamp is cool.)
3. Release the lamp from the locking device and remove it.
4. Replace the lamp with one having the identical lamp number or one identified as an acceptable substitute.
5. Close the lamp cover or panel.

The Keystone Effect

The most common mistake made when using the overhead projector is not having the projector at a 90 degree angle with the screen. This results in poor projection and a distorted image called the keystone effect or "keystoning." The keystone effect can be corrected by repositioning (1) the overhead projector, (2) the head assembly, or (3) the projection screen.

| **Vertical Distortion** | **Horizontal Distortion** | **Correct** |

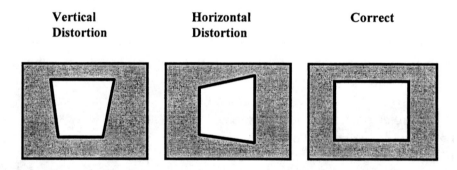

5.3 - Designing Overhead Transparencies

The first step in creating transparencies is designing their layout. The following 12 guidelines will produce transparencies that will be effective technology tools for teachers.

- Use one concept or theme per transparency.
- Use bold or block lettering that is easy to read.
- Use more than one letter size on each transparency.
- Use lines and white space to place emphasis on content.
- Use a horizontal or landscape orientation for frames.
- Use a horizontal lettering layout, not vertical.

- Place drawings off-center, using the "rule of thirds."
- Place headings at the top, either in the center or to the left side.
- Mix formal and informal balance when creating a series.
- Use color to create a mood and/or emphasize a point.
- Create a feeling of unity or oneness in the overall layout.
- Keep text to a minimum.

Materials For Making And Using Transparencies

Types of Transparency Film

There are a variety of transparency films available; each is designed to be compatible with one or more specific transparency production methods. The transparency making equipment may be damaged if an inappropriate film is used when making the transparency. The most common types of transparency film are:

- write-on transparency film
- transparency film for plain paper copiers
- transparency film for laser printers
- transparency film for ink jet printers
- film for infrared (thermal) transparency makers

Some transparency films are also available in various "weights." These include standard weight, medium weight, and heavy weight.

Colors of Transparency Film

In addition to the standard clear film, a variety of colored film sheets are available for many of the processes. These are more costly than the traditional clear film formats. Examples include:

- black image on clear film (traditional film)
- red, blue, green, yellow, or violet image on clear film
- yellow image on blue, red, green, or violet background

Transparency Markers

These are special markers that are specifically intended to be used when making overhead transparencies. They are labeled as "transparency markers." Some use water soluble ink and some use permanent ink. Unlike traditional permanent ink markers, transparency markers with permanent ink will allow their color to be projected.

41

Transparency Framing/Storing Options

Transparency frames can be made of heavy cardboard, thin sheet plastic, or heavy plastic. The cardboard frames are intended to have presentation notes written on the frame. The new "flip-frame" transparency protectors have a sleeve to store the transparency, flip-out borders for notes, and holes for storing in a 3-ring notebook. Transparencies can also be protected and stored in regular "plastic sheet protectors."

Instructional Technology Tools

Formats For Transparency Layout

Various formats can be used when planning the layout of an overhead transparency. The following layout designs represent some of the most common formats for presenting textual (words and/or numbers) material.

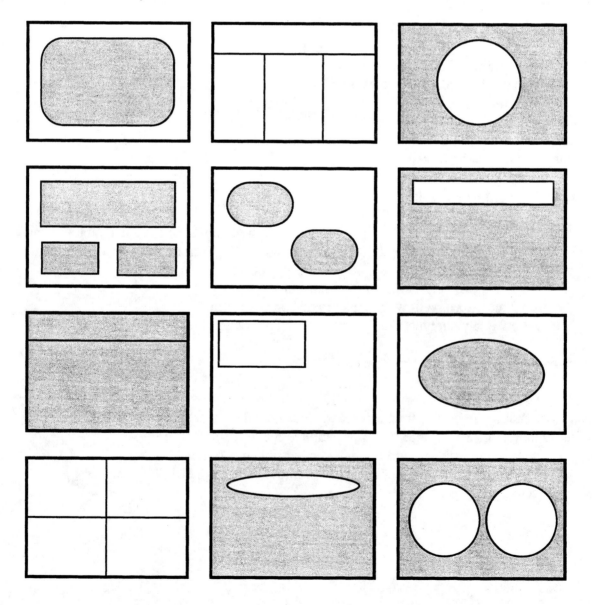

How To Make Overhead Transparencies

There are a number of different ways to make an overhead transparency. Three of the most common methods/categories are: (1) handmade transparencies, (2) transparencies made using a xerographic copying machine, and (3) computer generated and printed transparencies.

Handmade Transparencies

Handmade transparencies can either be done quickly or they can be extremely time consuming; plan first. Plain acetate film should be used for this method. (For an inexpensive alternative, use acetate sheet protectors for three-ring notebooks.)

Handmade lettering and drawings can be made with either permanent ink felt-tip markers or with special transparency markers. Do not use water soluble markers, as they will bead-up. Pointed markers are used for lines and broad-tip markers can be used to color in small shapes and to do broad-lined lettering. Coloring books, stencils, and magazines are an unlimited tracing library of both letters and objects for those who either are not artistically inclined or want to make the process go quicker.

Xerographic Copying Machine Transparencies

Transparencies made on xerographic copiers are extremely easy to produce. Place the master on the copier just as if you were going to make a paper copy. But instead of feeding paper into the machine, feed the recommended transparency material that is used in these machines. Some manufacturers make material especially for their copiers. However, most copiers will accept film labeled "For plain paper copiers." Check the film box before using any film, as the machine can be damaged if the incorrect film is used. One advantage of making transparencies on larger copiers is their ability to reduce and/or enlarge the copy of the original.

Computer Created / Laser or Ink Jet Printed Transparencies

A transparency master, as well as the actual transparency, can be created using a computer and a printer. The paper printout of a page designed on the computer and printed with a laser printer is the perfect master for making a transparency. However, the process can be shortened by designing the page on the computer screen, placing transparency material into the paper feed tray, and having the printout be on the actual transparency film. This may be done with a laser printer or an ink jet printer. (Only transparency film designated for the particular printer should be used. Incorrect film may damage the printer.)

Technology
Tools
for
Teachers

5.4 - Teaching with Transparencies

Overhead transparencies can be formatted to accommodate three different methods of presentation: (1) direct presentation, (2) progressive disclosure, and (3) overlay presentation. The transparency content will determine what format will be used when preparing and using the transparency.

Direct Presentation

Except for the fact that the transparency is either mounted in a transparency frame or placed in a plastic protector sheet, *direct presentation* is the use of a single transparency in the exact form it was produced. The frame or plastic sheet is used to protect and store the transparency.

Progressive Disclosure

Progressive disclosure is a name that includes many different techniques, all with the same intent--to display or disclose the information on the transparency a portion at a time or progressively. This technique is used when the content is part of a whole but the teacher wants to disclose the elements as they are explained. To achieve this, sections of the transparency are "masked." This can be simply done by covering all or some of the transparency with a sheet of paper and revealing the content as needed. However, for transparencies that are going to be used on a regular basis and for a more professional presentation, the following approaches can be used:

Overlay Presentation

Overlay presentation is used when specific information dealing with a concept is to be presented, a portion at a time. Each element is placed on a separate transparency, with the entire set hinged to the lead transparency. The transparencies are then "folded-in" or "overlayed" as they are used. There are two types of overlays: Fixed Sequence Overlays and Random Sequence Overlays.

Fixed Sequence Overlays have two or more transparencies all hinged to the frame and coordinated with the main transparency mounted in the frame. Material is presented in the predetermined sequence of the overlays.

Random Sequence Overlays have two, three, or four transparencies hinged to the frame. Since each transparency overlay is independent of the other, overlays of this type can be used in any combination and sequence the presenter chooses.

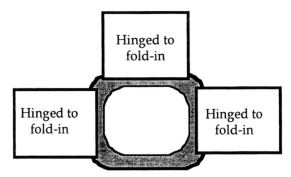

How To Use Transparencies To Resize Art Work

The combination of an overhead transparency and an overhead projector can save the teacher a considerable amount of time when art work is needed for bulletin boards, posters, outlines for wall murals, and other such instances. Existing art work can easily be reduced or enlarged in the following manner:

1. Select the item you want to use (sketch in a newspaper, map in a textbook, picture in a magazine, outline in a workbook, line drawing in a coloring book, etc.).
2. Make a xerographic copy of the artwork. Do not be concerned if there are elements around or with the drawing that you do not want to use copy the entire section so the part you do want is included in the copy.
3. Make a transparency from the copy you just made. Again, do not be concerned if items are copied that you do not want.
4. Tape the poster board, paper, or other material you want to have the final art work on to a wall. If you were creating a wall mural you would use the actual wall as your surface.
5. Place the transparency on an overhead projector and project the image onto the poster board, paper, or wall.
6. Move the overhead projector closer to, or further away from, the paper until the projected image is the size you want. Adjust the focus as you near the desired size.
7. Using a pencil, marker, etc., trace the outline of those parts of the image that you want to use.
8. Complete the line drawing of the art work to meet your needs.

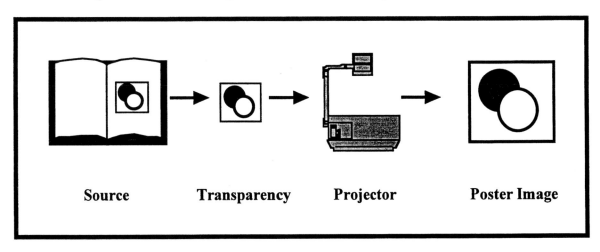

Source   **Transparency**   **Projector**   **Poster Image**

5.5 - Visual Presenters

Visual presenters are also called document cameras, presentation cameras, and visualizers. They are used in traditional instructional settings as well as in conjunction with video conferencing systems. Their wide appeal is due to the variety of materials that can be shown with this technology. These include all paper documents (books, periodicals, written assignments, newspaper clippings, etc.), transparencies, photographs, 35mm slides, and realia (3-dimensional objects ranging from small tools and coins to plants or a live worm).

A typical visual presenter consists of (1) a stage on which the object is placed, (2) a video camera mounted above the stage, (3) directional lights that illuminate the stage from above, and (4) a light built into the stage that allows it to function as an overhead projector for transparencies and slides.

How To Use Visual Presenters

The visual presenter is an input technology and therefore must be coupled with an output technology such as a television monitor or a video projector. Due to the variety of models, the operator's manual for the specific model being used should be consulted. The following are general directions for the two basic uses: presenting opaque materials and presenting transparent materials.

To Present Opaque Materials

Opaque materials are items that light will not project through. This includes books, periodicals, drawings, and all three-dimensional objects such as tools, coins, small plants, insects, etc.

1. Unlock the column arm and set the camera head in position (if required for the model being used).
2. Plug-in the power cord.
3. Connect the visual presenter to the selected output device--TV monitor or video projector. (See the operator's manual.)
4. Turn on the output device.
5. Turn on the visual presenter.
6. Turn on the "directional lights."
7. Place the object to be presented on the "stage."
8. Adjust the "focus" and "zoom" to achieve the optimum image.
9. USE the visual presenter to present opaque objects.
10. Reverse the steps for "shut-down."

To Present Transparent Materials

The most common type of transparent materials are overhead transparencies. These can be either commercial or teacher-made.

1. Unlock the column arm and set the camera head in position (if required for the model being used).
2. Plug-in the power cord.
3. Connect the visual presenter to the selected output device--TV monitor or video projector. (See the operator's manual for the model being used.)
4. Turn on the output device.
5. Turn on the visual presenter.
6. Turn on the "stage light."
7. Place the object to be presented on the "stage."
8. Adjust the "focus" and "zoom" to achieve the optimum image.
9. USE the visual presenter to present opaque objects.
10. Reverse the steps for "shut-down."

Compact and Portable Visual Presenters

The standard visual presenter discussed above is the model most frequently used in schools. It can be a permanent attachment to an instructional counter or desk, or it can have a handle to allow it to be moved from one location to another. In recent years, a number of compact and portable models have become available. These are generally less costly and allow for easy movement from one location to another.

5.6 - Activities

• Activity One •

Design two transparencies for a lesson you will teach. Use a different process to make each of the transparencies. Compare the advantages and disadvantages of each process.

• Activity Two •

Design a transparency that uses progressive disclosure or overlay presentation as the method of presentation. Use the transparency to make a brief presentation to the class.

• Activity Three •

Using the procedure in "How to Use Transparencies to Resize Art Work," select an image from a textbook or a periodical and transfer that image to a poster that is approximately 16" x 24" in size.

Tool

6

Content Area Standards and Technology Standards

6.1 - Introduction

The current emphasis on standards-based instruction stems from a 1983 report from the National Commission on Excellence in Education titled *A Nation at Risk: The Imperative for Education Reform*. In the years following this report, content area standards were developed by the various national subject-matter organizations. This movement was replicated on the state level with the issuance of content area standards developed by state departments of education. Educators should be cognizant of the standards mandated by their state department of education, as well as the standards set forth by the professional organization(s) in the content area. These standards set forth the knowledge, skills, and dispositions that are essential at each grade level. Concurrent with this development was the creation of technology standards for students and teachers by the International Society for Technology in Education (ISTE), the largest international, non-profit organization in the area of educational technology

6.2 - Professional Associations

Professional associations exist for all of the content areas. In many cases these associations have developed a set of content area standards that have been adopted by the educational community. In other instances, the association has developed guidelines to address the content area. The following list identifies the leading professional associations in the educational community that have developed standards or guidelines to address content coverage.

- **American Alliance for Health, Physical Education, Recreation and Dance (AAHPERD)**
www.aahperd.org
> The largest organization of professionals supporting and assisting those involved in physical education, leisure, fitness, dance, health promotion, and education and all specialties related to achieving a healthy lifestyle.

- **American Association of Family and Consumer Sciences (AAFCS)**
www.aafcs.org
> The only national forum where K-12 teachers, university educators and corporate executives collaborate to improve the quality of individual and family life.

- **American Council on the Teaching of Foreign Languages (ACTFL)**
www.actfl.org
> The only national organization dedicated to the improvement and expansion of the teaching and learning of all languages at all levels of instruction throughout the United States.

- **Association for Career and Technical Education (ACTE)**
www.acteonline.org
> The largest national education association dedicated to the advancement of education that prepares youth and adults for careers.

- **Association for the Advancement of Computing in Education (AACE)**
  www.aace.org
  > An international, educational, and professional organization dedicated to the advancement of the knowledge, theory, and quality of learning and teaching at all levels with information technology.

- **Council for Exceptional Children (CEC)**
  www.cec.sped.org
  > The largest international professional organization dedicated to improving educational outcomes for individuals with exceptionalities, students with disabilities, and/or the gifted.

- **Family and Consumer Sciences Education Organization (FCSEA)**
  www.cwu.edu/~fandcs/fcsea
  > An organization of family and consumer sciences educators and others associated with or interested in family and consumer sciences instruction in schools and colleges.

- **International Reading Association (IRA)**
  www.reading.org
  > The world's leading organization of literacy professionals involved in teaching reading to learners of all ages.

- **International Society for Technology in Education (ISTE)**
  www.iste.org
  > A professional organization with a worldwide membership of leaders and potential leaders in educational technology.

- **International Technology Education Association (ITEA)**
  www.iteaconnect.org/A6.html
  > The largest professional educational association, principal voice, and information clearinghouse devoted to enhancing technology education through technology, innovation, design, and engineering experiences at the K-12 school levels.

- **Music Teachers National Association (MTNA)**
  www.mtna.org
  > The mission of MTNA is to advance the value of music study and music making to society and to support the professionalism of music teachers.

- **National Art Education Association (NAEA)**
  www.naea-reston.org
  > NAEA promotes art education through professional development, service, advancement of knowledge, and leadership.

- **National Association for Bilingual Education (NABE)**
  www.nabe.org
  > The National Association for Bilingual Education is the only professional organization at the national level wholly devoted to representing both English language learners and bilingual education professionals.

- **National Association for the Education of Young Children (NAEYC)**
  www.naeyc.org
  > NAEYC is dedicated to improving the well-being of all young children, with particular focus on the quality of educational and developmental services for all children from birth through age 8.

- **National Association for Gifted Children (NAGC)**
  www.nagc.org
  > An organization of parents, teachers, educators, other professionals, and community leaders who unite to address the unique needs of children and youth with demonstrated gifts and talents, as well as those children who may be able to develop their talent potential with appropriate educational experiences.

- **National Association for Music Education (MENC)**
  www.menc.org
  > The mission of MENC, The National Association for Music Education, is to advance music education by encouraging the study and making of music by all.

- **National Business Education Association (NBEA)**
  www.nbea.org
  > The nation's largest professional organization devoted exclusively to serving individuals and groups engaged in instruction, administration, research, and dissemination of information for and about business.

- **National Council of Teachers of English (NCTE)**
  www.ncte.org
  > NCTE is devoted to improving the teaching and learning of English and the language arts at all levels of education.

- **National Council of Teachers of Mathematics (NCTM)**
  www.nctm.org
  > As the world's largest mathematics education organization, NCTM is a public voice of mathematics education, providing vision, leadership, and professional development to support teachers in ensuring mathematics learning of the highest quality for all students.

- **National Council for the Social Studies (NCSS)**
  www.socialstudies.org
  > The largest association in the country devoted solely to social studies education.

• **National Science Teachers Association (NSTA)**
www.nsta.org
> The largest organization in the world committed to promoting excellence and innovation in science teaching and learning for all.

• **Teachers of English to Speakers of Other Languages (TESOL)**
www.tesol.org
> TESOL is a global education association whose mission is to ensure excellence in English language teaching to speakers of other languages.

6.3 – National Educational Technology Standards for Students

The primary goal of the ISTE NETS Project is to enable stakeholders in PreK-12 education to develop national standards for educational uses of technology that facilitate school improvement in the United States. The NETS Project will work to define standards for students, integrating curriculum technology, technology support, and standards for student assessment and evaluation of technology use. (NETS home page: cnets.iste.org)

The *National Educational Technology Standards for Students* (NETS•S), the *Profiles for Technology Literate Students,* and the *National Educational Standards for Teachers* (NETS•T) are provided in this chapter. *Profiles for Technology Literate Teachers* can be found at ISTE's Web site: cnets.iste.org/teachers/t_profiles.html.

[The content in sections 6.3, 6.4, and 6.5 are reproductions of material found at the ISTE Web site (www.iste.org).]

The National Educational Technology Standards for Students is designed to provide teachers, technology planners, teacher preparation institutions, and educational decision-makers with frameworks and standards to guide them in establishing enriched learning environments supported by technology.

The technology foundation standards for students are divided into six broad categories. Standards within each category are to be introduced, reinforced, and mastered by students. These categories provide a framework for linking performance indicators within the *Profiles for Technology Literate Students* to the standards. Teachers can use these standards and profiles as guidelines for planning technology-based activities in which students achieve success in learning, communication, and life skills.

Technology Foundation Standards for Students

1. Basic operations and concepts
   - Students demonstrate a sound understanding of the nature and operation of technology systems.
   - Students are proficient in the use of technology.

2. Social, ethical, and human issues
   - Students understand the ethical, cultural, and societal issues related to technology.
   - Students practice responsible use of technology systems, information, and software.
   - Students develop positive attitudes toward technology uses that support lifelong learning, collaboration, personal pursuits, and productivity.

3. Technology productivity tools
   - Students use technology tools to enhance learning, increase productivity, and promote creativity.
   - Students use productivity tools to collaborate in constructing technology-enhanced models, prepare publications, and produce other creative works.

4. Technology communications tools
   - Students use telecommunications to collaborate, publish, and interact with peers, experts, and other audiences.
   - Students use a variety of media and formats to communicate information and ideas effectively to multiple audiences.

5. Technology research tools
   - Students use technology to locate, evaluate, and collect information from a variety of sources.
   - Students use technology tools to process data and report results.
   - Students evaluate and select new information resources and technological innovations based on the appropriateness for specific tasks.

6. Technology problem-solving and decision-making tools
   - Students use technology resources for solving problems and making informed decisions.
   - Students employ technology in the development of strategies for solving problems in the real world.

6.4 - Profiles for Technology Literate Students

The Profiles for Technology Literate Students provide performance indicators describing the technology competence students should exhibit upon completion of the following grade ranges:

- Grades PreK - 2   - Grades 6 - 8

- Grades 3 - 5   - Grades 9 - 12

These profiles are indicators of achievement at certain stages in PreK-12 education. They assume that technology skills are developed by coordinated activities that support learning throughout a student's education. These skills are to be introduced, reinforced, and finally mastered, and thus, integrated into an individual's personal learning and social framework. They represent essential, realistic, and attainable goals for lifelong learning and a productive citizenry. The standards and performance indicators are based on input and feedback from educational technology experts as well as parents, teachers, and curriculum experts. In addition, they reflect information collected from professional literature and local, state, and national documents.

[Numbers in parentheses following each performance indicator refer to the standards category to which the performance is linked.]

GRADES PreK - 2

Prior to completion of Grade 2, students will:

1. Use input devices (e.g., mouse, keyboard, remote control) and output devices (e.g., monitor, printer) to successfully operate computers, VCRs, audiotapes, and other technologies. (1)
2. Use a variety of media and technology resources for directed and independent learning activities. (1, 3)
3. Communicate about technology using developmentally appropriate and accurate terminology. (1)
4. Use developmentally appropriate multimedia resources (e.g., interactive books, educational software, elementary multimedia encyclopedias) to support learning. (1)
5. Work cooperatively and collaboratively with peers, family members, and others when using technology in the classroom. (2)
6. Demonstrate positive social and ethical behaviors when using technology. (2)
7. Practice responsible use of technology systems and software. (2)
8. Create developmentally appropriate multimedia products with support from teachers, family members, or student partners. (3)
9. Use technology resources (e.g., puzzles, logical thinking programs, writing tools, digital cameras, drawing tools) for problem solving, communication, and illustration of thoughts, ideas, and stories. (3, 4, 5, 6)
10. Gather information and communicate with others using telecommunications, with support from teachers, family members, or student partners. (4)

GRADES 3 - 5

Prior to completion of Grade 5, students will:

1. Use keyboards and other common input and output devices (including adaptive devices when necessary) efficiently and effectively. (1)
2. Discuss common uses of technology in daily life and the advantages and disadvantages those uses provide. (1, 2)
3. Discuss basic issues related to responsible use of technology and information and describe personal consequences of inappropriate use. (2)
4. Use general purpose productivity tools and peripherals to support personal productivity, remediate skill deficits, and facilitate learning throughout the curriculum. (3)
5. Use technology tools (e.g., multimedia, authoring, presentation, Web tools, digital cameras, scanners) for individual and collaborative writing, communication, and publishing activities to create knowledge products for audiences inside and outside the classroom. (3, 4)
6. Use telecommunications efficiently to access remote information, communicate with others in support of direct and independent learning, and pursue personal interests. (4)
7. Use telecommunications and online resources (e.g., e-mail, online discussions, Web environments) to participate in collaborative problem-solving activities for the purpose of developing solutions or products for audiences inside and outside the classroom. (4, 5)
8. Use technology resources (e.g., calculators, data collection probes, videos, educational software) for problem solving, self-directed learning, and extended learning activities. (5, 6)

9. Determine which technology is useful and select the appropriate tool(s) and technology resources to address a variety of tasks and problems. (5, 6)
10. Evaluate the accuracy, relevance, appropriateness, comprehensiveness, and bias of electronic information sources. (6)

GRADES 6 - 8

Prior to completion of Grade 8, students will:

1. Apply strategies for identifying and solving routine hardware and software problems that occur during everyday use. (1)
2. Demonstrate knowledge of current changes in information technologies and the effect those changes have on the workplace and society. (2)
3. Exhibit legal and ethical behaviors when using information and technology, and discuss consequences of misuse. (2)
4. Use content-specific tools, software, and simulations (e.g., environmental probes, graphing calculators, exploratory environments, Web tools) to support learning and research. (3, 5)
5. Apply productivity/multimedia tools and peripherals to support personal productivity, group collaboration, and learning throughout the curriculum. (3, 6)
6. Design, develop, publish, and present products (e.g., Web pages, videotapes) using technology resources that demonstrate and communicate curriculum concepts to audiences inside and outside the classroom. (4, 5, 6)
7. Collaborate with peers, experts, and others using telecommunications and collaborative tools to investigate curriculum-related problems, issues, and information, and to develop solutions or products for audiences inside and outside the classroom. (4, 5)
8. Select and use appropriate tools and technology resources to accomplish a variety of tasks and solve problems. (5, 6)
9. Demonstrate an understanding of concepts underlying applications to learning and problem solving. (1, 6)
10. Research and evaluate the accuracy, relevance appropriateness, comprehensiveness, and bias of electronic information sources concerning real-world problems. (2, 5, 6)

GRADES 9 - 12

Prior to completion of Grade 12, students will:

1. Identify capabilities and limitations of contemporary and emerging technology resources and assess the potential of these systems and services to address personal, lifelong learning, and workplace needs. (2)
2. Make informed choices among technology systems, resources, and services. (1, 2)
3. Analyze advantages and disadvantages of widespread use and reliance on technology in the workplace and in society as a whole. (2)
4. Demonstrate and advocate for legal and ethical behaviors among peers, family, and community regarding the use of technology and information. (2)
5. Use technology tools and resources for managing and communicating personal/professional information (e.g., finances, schedules, addresses, purchases, correspondence). (3, 4)
6. Evaluate technology-based options, including distance and distributed education, for lifelong learning. (5)
7. Routinely and efficiently use online information resources to meet needs for collaboration, research, publications, communications, and productivity. (4, 5, 6)
8. Select and apply technology tools for research, information analysis, problem-solving, and decision-making in content learning. (4, 5)

9. Investigate and apply expert systems, intelligent agents, and simulations in real-world situations. (3, 5, 6)
10. Collaborate with peers, experts, and others to contribute to a content-related knowledge base by using technology to compile, synthesize, produce, and disseminate information, models, and other creative works. (4, 5, 6)

6.5 - National Educational Technology Standards for Teachers

Building on the NETS for Students, the ISTE NETS for Teachers (NETS•T), which focus on preservice teacher education, define the fundamental concepts, knowledge, skills, and attitudes for applying technology in educational settings. All candidates seeking certification or endorsements in teacher preparation should meet these educational technology standards. It is the responsibility of faculty across the university and at cooperating schools to provide opportunities for teacher candidates to meet these standards.

The six standards areas with performance indicators listed below are designed to be general enough to be customized to fit state, university, or district guidelines and yet specific enough to define the scope of the topic. Performance indicators for each standard provide specific outcomes to be measured when developing a set of assessment tools. The standards and the performance indicators also provide guidelines for teachers currently in the classroom.

I. TECHNOLOGY OPERATIONS AND CONCEPTS
Teachers demonstrate a sound understanding of technology operations and concepts.
Teachers:
    A. demonstrate introductory knowledge, skills, and understanding of concepts related to technology (as described in the ISTE National Education Technology Standards for Students).
    B. demonstrate continual growth in technology knowledge and skills to stay abreast of current and emerging technologies.

II. PLANNING AND DESIGNING LEARNING ENVIRONMENTS AND EXPERIENCES
Teachers plan and design effective learning environments and experiences supported by technology. Teachers:
    A. design developmentally appropriate learning opportunities that apply technology-enhanced instructional strategies to support the diverse needs of learners.
    B. apply current research on teaching and learning with technology when planning learning environments and experiences.
    C. identify and locate technology resources and evaluate them for accuracy and suitability.
    D. plan for the management of technology resources within the context of learning activities.
    E. plan strategies to manage student learning in a technology enhanced environment.

III. TEACHING, LEARNING, AND THE CURRICULUM
Teachers implement curriculum plans, that include methods and strategies for applying technology to maximize student learning. Teachers:
    A. facilitate technology-enhanced experiences that address content standards and student technology standards.
    B. use technology to support learner-centered strategies that address the diverse needs of students.
    C. apply technology to develop students' higher order skills and creativity.
    D. manage student learning activities in a technology enhanced environment.

57

IV.   **ASSESSMENT AND EVALUATION**
Teachers apply technology to facilitate a variety of effective assessment and evaluation strategies. Teachers:
   A.   apply technology in assessing student learning of subject matter using a variety of assessment techniques.
   B.   use technology resources to collect and analyze data, interpret results, and communicate findings to improve instructional practice and maximize student learning.
   C.   apply multiple methods of evaluation to determine students' appropriate use of technology resources for learning, communication, and productivity.

V.   **PRODUCTIVITY AND PROFESSIONAL PRACTICE**
Teachers use technology to enhance their productivity and professional practice. Teachers:
   A.   use technology resources to engage in ongoing professional development and lifelong learning.
   B.   continually evaluate and reflect on professional practice to make informed decisions regarding the use of technology in support of student learning.
   C.   apply technology to increase productivity.
   D.   use technology to communicate and collaborate with peers, parents, and the larger community in order to nurture student learning.

VI.   **SOCIAL, ETHICAL, LEGAL, AND HUMAN ISSUES**
Teachers understand the social, ethical, legal, and human issues surrounding the use of technology in PK-12 schools and apply those principles in practice. Teachers:
   A.   model and teach legal and ethical practice related to technology use.
   B.   apply technology resources to enable and empower learners with diverse backgrounds, characteristics, and abilities.
   C.   identify and use technology resources that affirm diversity.
   D.   promote safe and healthy use of technology resources.
   E.   facilitate equitable access to technology resources for all students.

6.6 - Activities

• Activity One •

Select a professional organization from those identified in section 6.2 and go to their Web site. Examine the online materials available and identify three resources that will be of value to you as a teacher. Using this information, write a two-page (word processed, double-spaced) report that describes the resources and identifies when and how you could use them.

• Activity Two •

Read the "NETS for Teachers" contained in section 6.5. Write a one-page, double-spaced reflection addressing how these standards would impact on your actions as a teacher. Your reflection should include three sections: Description, Analysis, and Future Impact.

Tool

7

The Internet

7.1 - Introduction

The Internet is a network of computers around the world. It began as an experiment in the late 1960s when the United States Department of Defense, doing military research and needing to access and share information with various units and universities, developed a communication network. In the 1970s, universities and research institutions joined the network, with popularity becoming worldwide during the 1990s. Today, the Internet has permeated every facet of our lives in every corner of the world.

It is often said that the Internet cannot be defined. It is not a place or thing, it is not owned by any person or group, and there is no one in charge. It is a global collection of people and computers linked by cables and telephone lines, all freely exchanging information. This cluster of interconnected networks worldwide gives millions of users access to people, as well as a constantly changing collection of documents, resources, and databases.

The terms Internet and World Wide Web (WWW) are often used interchangeably. They are not the same. The WWW is a part of the Internet, emerging in the early 1990s. E-mail is another component we find in schools and homes today.

7.2 - Connecting to the Internet

Use of the Internet is available to anyone who has a computer with a modem or Ethernet card and connection to the Internet. The higher the GHz speed and RAM (Random Access Memory) of the computer, the better it will function on the Internet.

The speed of accessing the Internet is dependent upon the type of connection one has to the Internet. Dial-up service is available via a computer modem and a connection over a telephone line. This is the slowest connection and ties up the telephone line while using the Internet. If using a modem, be sure the number you call is local and has unlimited minutes. DSL (Digital Subscriber Line) and cable TV deliver the Internet with higher access speeds. A modem is connected to the computer and either the telephone or cable line, resulting in speeds more than ten times faster than a 56K modem. These connections also allow the house phone line to be accessible while the Internet is in use. In addition to speed, another advantage is that the Internet can always be active. You can be connected to the Internet whenever your computer is on.

Any of these connections require a monthly contract with a service provider. Ease of use, speed, accessibility, and the type of services offered vary with providers and connections. Prices for dial-up service are $10 - $20 per month, while higher speed connections could be in the vicinity of $40 - $50 per month. Other considerations are the number of e-mail accounts you receive, space provided for a Web page, customer support, and computer requirements.

Schools are usually connected over networks, allowing them high-speed access to the Internet (using Ethernet cards and often wireless connections).

7.3 - Browsing the World Wide Web

Once the computer has a connection to access the Internet, browser software is needed to access and view the Web pages. Most computers come with browser software installed.

The two major browsers are *Netscape Navigator* (a part of *Netscape Communicator*™) and *Microsoft® Internet Explorer*. PCs usually come with *Explorer* installed; however, there is a *Windows* version of *Netscape*. There are also versions of *Netscape* and *Explorer* available for Macintosh (no new versions of *Explorer* will be made for Macintosh). Newer browsers are *Safari*, which comes installed on Apple Macintosh computers, and *FireFox*, available for both *Windows* and *Macintosh OSX*. Software downloads are free from their Web sites. Doing a search for Web browsers will identify many others that are available.

Which should you use? It is a personal choice. They are all similar and each has advantages and disadvantages. Test them out – Web pages usually appear differently in each browser.

When a browser opens, a Web page appears. At first it is the browser's home page. You can set this to any page you want under *Preferences*. In the example below, Rowan University has been selected as the home page.

Toolbar Buttons and Menu Items [*Microsoft Internet Explorer*]

Toolbar Buttons:

> *Back:* Go back one page in the viewed sequence.
> *Forward:* Go forward one page in the viewed sequence.
> *Stop:* Click to stop loading a Web page.
> *Refresh:* Update the page if there have been any changes since last viewed.
> *Home:* Go back to the home page (the first one seen when the browser begins).
>> (This page can be set to your choice under *Preferences*.)
> *AutoFill:* Helps to fill out forms.
> *Print:* Print the current Web page selection.
> *Mail:* Opens an e-mail program.

Menu Items:

> *Window-History:* Lists Web sites visited in the last few days/weeks.
> *Go:* Lists sites most recently visited; another way to go back.
> *Favorites/Bookmarks:* A list of favorite sites; bookmarked to return to easily.

Address Bar

Each Web page has a Web address or a URL (Uniform Resource Locator). It must be entered exactly or the Web site will not be found. The majority begin with *http://* (Hypertext Transfer Protocol): a set of rules and procedures that allow Web sites to work. These are the same for all computers and connections. When entering an address, it is not necessary to enter the *http://* in the address; it is understood. The Web address for this book is users.rowan.edu/~levy/15. (Note: not all Web addresses begin with *www*.) The Web address is entered in the Address Bar (also termed the Location or the URL). Enter the address, then click on *Go* or press the *Enter/Return* key. The site for the address entered should appear in the browser. Some browsers also do not require the *www* and *.com* for .com addresses. If the address ends in *.com*. you can just enter the Web name, such as *google*, instead of www.google.com.

Access hyperlinks used in this book at: users.rowan.edu/~levy/15

Bookmarks/Favorites

Any time you locate a site you want to return to at a later time, add a Bookmark (*Netscape*) or Favorite (*Internet Explorer*). It will be stored in a listing in the menu bar for access at a later time. Bookmarks/Favorites can be organized in folders by using *Edit Bookmarks* (*Netscape*) or *Organize Favorites* (*Internet Explorer*). The Web site for this book is (users.rowan.edu/~levy/15) contains hyperlinks to all sites mentioned in this book. Bookmark this site for easy access to these hyperlinks.

Saving and Printing Sites

Being connected to the Internet is not the only way to access the information found there. Some alternative ways are:

Downloading Web Pages

To view Web pages at a later time when you are not connected to the Internet, pages can be saved. To save a file, go to *File: Save As: Source (or Text)*. Source saves the entire page as it looks on the Internet; text saves only the text portion.

Sending Files

Some browsers have an option to send pages (look under *File* in the Menu Bar). This allows you to retain the Web address by sending it to an e-mail address. (For example. if you are working at school, and find a great site, send it to your home e-mail instead of copying the address.)

Printing

Most pages can be printed with the print command. To determine where the page breaks are, go to *Print Preview*. Some documents allow you to highlight the text, copy it, and paste it into a word processing document. Graphics can also be copied to documents [see Tool 12: Drawing Tools and Clip Art]. If the site is wide (you cannot see all of it without scrolling to the right on the monitor), the entire page will not fit on the paper vertically (two pages will be printed that need to be placed together to read all of the page). When this happens, go to *File; Page Setup*; change the page orientation to print horizontally *(landscape)*.

PDF Documents

Documents on the Internet that are meant to be printed are saved in Portable Document Format (*PDF*). *PDF* formats the text to be printed in a book-like format. Examples include user guides, price lists, articles, and other documents that are meant to be printed for reading off the Internet. To view and print the document, the software *Adobe Acrobat Reader* must be installed on the computer. This can be downloaded for free from the Internet [www.adobe.com]. Using *Acrobat Reader*, the document may be saved to the hard drive, desktop, or a disk. The file can then be opened and printed in a readable format.

7.4 - Communicating on the Internet

There is always a need to communicate with other people - colleagues, parents, students, or friends - and exchange information. Frequently, however, problems arise: you do not have time, the other party is not home, now is not a good time to talk, etc. This can be solved by asynchronous communication - sending messages, reading them, and replying to them when the time is available (and you are ready). On the Internet, e-mail, newsgroups, and mailing lists are a few of the tools for asynchronous communication. Other tools, such as chat rooms and instant messaging, are synchronous - messages are sent and received at the same time.

E-Mail (Electronic Mail)

 Of the various tools for communication via the Internet, e-mail is the most common for teachers and students. Through e-mail, messages and files are transmitted via a computer network, allowing you to send, receive and store messages on your computer. E-mail messages not only contain text; graphics, photos, audio, video, computer files, and electronic cards can also be a part of a message. You can compose messages, reply to others, forward messages, store, print, and delete messages.

For anyone with an Internet connection, e-mail is free. You can communicate with friends and colleagues in any state or country. In addition to correspondence with those you know, students can have key pals, while teachers can share ideas and discuss problems with others in their field.

Most browsers, Internet service providers, and portals provide free e-mail accounts. You can have one or many. It is a good idea to have different accounts for different purposes: personal, professional, school, etc. An advantage to free accounts from Web portals is that mail can be checked at any time from any computer via the Internet.

E-Mail Address

An e-mail address is needed to receive messages. The mail server for your e-mail places your received messages in a box until you retrieve them. Each address contains specific components so that the mail is sent to the correct mail server.

In the address, each user has a user name (provided with the account) and a domain name (where the mail is sent). The user name and domain name are separated by the @ sign. The domain name ends in a three-letter abbreviation identifying the organization sponsoring the mail server. A few of these abbreviations are: *.edu*=educational, *.gov*=government, *.org*=organization, etc. An example is Lynne Levy at Rowan University, an educational institution: levy@rowan.edu. For addresses outside of the United States, an additional two-letter country abbreviation is added at the end.

K-12 schools with direct mail have their addresses terminating in k12.state.country. A fictitious example of this would be if Lynne Levy taught at Rowan High School in Glassboro, New Jersey. This address might be: levy@rhs.k12.nj.us.

In the Classroom: E-Pals/KeyPals

Schools can set up free, safe e-mail accounts for students. Sites offering these free accounts have filters that block junk mail. Some also block inappropriate language, while others allow teachers to review students' address books. Two examples of these are *Think.com* and *Gaggle.net*.

Using e-mail in the classroom, students can:
- make new friends
- learn about other towns, cities, and countries
- exchange photos
- collaborate on stories and projects
- do research on projects
- communicate with their teachers and their peers

Using e-mail, these exchanges can be with someone in the same town or in another country. Since a keyboard, not a pen, is used, those they communicate with are termed *key pals* or *e-pals* (electronic).

There are a variety of sites on the Internet where the teacher can go to find key pals for students. *Epals.com®* (www.epals.com) is the largest, connecting over 100,000 classrooms and six million students and educators in 191 countries. Students can participate in cross-cultural learning and classroom-to-classroom projects. In addition to e-mail, photographs, and sound and video clips, show the students what life is like in other countries. Another example is *IECC* (www.iecc.org) (Intercultural E-mail Classroom Connections). At this site, teachers link with partners in other cultures and countries for e-mail connections and project exchanges.

Teachers can go to *Teachnet* (www.teachnet.com/t2t) to keep connected with other educators around the world. Those involved exchange ideas pertaining to the K-12 classroom through daily e-mail, a daily e-mail digest, and weekly announcements.

E-mail Attachments

Attachments are enclosures such as photos or computer files. To send an attachment, click on *Attach* (usually a paperclip) at the top (or side) of the screen; then locate the file on the computer to be attached. Photos must be in the *.jpeg* format.

It is a good idea to send the attachment to yourself first to be sure it works. Computer files must be compatible with the recipient's computer. For example, a file sent which was composed using *Word* can only be opened with *Word* on the receiving computer. Be sure to include the extension, such as *.doc* for this example. Viruses are often sent through attachments on e-mail. Never open an attachment if you do not know the sender of the message.

Address Books

An address book is included with most e-mail programs. This allows you to store frequently used addresses, along with other data about the person. Distribution lists can be created from the addresses to send the same letter to multiple individuals (e.g.: a list of all students in your class). By choosing a specific list, the same message would be sent to everyone on the list.

Chatting and Instant Messaging

Chatting and instant messaging take place in real-time when users are online. Chat rooms are virtual areas where people meet and communicate. Areas are topic-specific with two or more people communicating at any one time. On the Internet, real names are not exchanged and caution must be used to be sure real identities, especially of children, are not revealed. While many chat rooms have poor reputations, others such as *KidsCom®* (www.kidscom.com), are designed for communication among children. Your Rowan professors can set up chat rooms within WebCT for group discussions.

Instant messaging (provided free by *AOL's Instant Messenger™*, *MSN® Messenger*, Macintosh's *iChat®*, and others) allows you to write messages back and forth to friends whenever you and the friend are online at the same time. Some also support video and voice conversations. *TaskStream* includes this feature, allowing you to communicate with others while online, asking questions and getting directions.

WebLogs (Blogs)

Blogs are online journals in the form of a Web page. While not a true form of Internet communication, they are Web pages whereby individuals post information. The person maintaining the page is a *blogger*, while the activity of updating the page is called *blogging*. Some types of pages are just for the *blogger* to post information, while others are for discussions. *MyOwnJournal*, *Blogger*™, and *LiveJournal*™ are three examples of free online journals. Blogs encourage students to express themselves, share thoughts and ideas, and write to other students.

7.5 - Internet Terminology

An understanding of the following additional terms will make you more conversant regarding the use of the Internet.

Address: location of a site on the Web.

Domain Name: a unique name assigned to a site, such as *google.com*.

FTP (File Transfer Protocol): a way of transferring electronic files (software, files, pictures, sounds) through the Internet.

Hypertext: a type of document that allows links to other documents.

Hypertext (Hot) Links: words, phrases or graphics that connect to another page on the Web site or any other site.

HTML (Hypertext Markup Language: the standardized coding language used to create hypertext documents on the WWW.

HTTP (Hypertext Transport Protocol): a communications protocol; used to move WWW documents on the Internet.

Link: an underlined word, phrase, or picture on a Web page; selecting the link takes you to a related page.

Plug-in: software programs, normally downloaded from the Internet, that extend the capabilities of the Web browser. Some come with the browser, others need to be downloaded (free). They usually extend the functionality of the browser for graphics, sound, and multimedia.

Portal: a Web site that offers a variety of services from one location, such as a search engine, news, weather, sports, stocks, maps, e-mail, chat rooms, yellow pages, shopping, and more. Home pages of browsers and search engines are common portals. A portal can be chosen as your home page that comes up each time the browser begins.

URL (Uniform Resource Locator): an Internet address; used to identify locations on the Web.

7.6 - Activities

• Activity One •

Go to Think.com and Gaggle.net. Explore these sites to learn about the features of their free e-mail accounts. Subscribe to each. Compare and contrast their features and ease of use.

• Activity Two •

Go to *Epals.com* (www.epals.com) and *IECC* (www.iecc.org). Explore these sites to learn about connecting your students with students in other countries. What does each site have to offer you for your classroom? How can your students participate in their projects?

• Activity Three •

Go to *Teachnet* (www.teachnet.com/t2t). Subscribe to their daily e-mail digest and weekly announcements. Follow these postings for three weeks. Report your findings.

Tool
8

Search Engines
and the
World Wide Web

8.1 - Introduction

Since the World Wide Web consists of several billion Web pages, locating what you want can be a problem. Search engines are software programs that help you find the information you need. Most search engines send *spiders* or *robots* out on the Web to find key words, bringing them back and placing them in a large database of terms. When you enter search terms, the database is searched for your key words. There are thousands of search engines; some are general, and some are for very specific searches. Not all searching can be done from common search engines such as *Google*™. Finding the right search engine for your purpose can be difficult. Once you have located the appropriate search engine, you need a good searching strategy.

8.2 - Types of Search Engines

Regular Search Engines

When users of the World Wide Web talk about using a search engine, they are usually referring to a regular search engine such as *Google*. In recent years, *Google* has become synonymous with searching the Web. One "Googles" to find information. In addition to basic searching, *Google* has a number of features on the main tool bar. A few of these are:

- *I'm Feeling Lucky*™: a button on the main search page that automatically takes you to the first Web page returned for your query.
- *Images:* billions of images (photographs, clip art) to search and use (check for permissions).
- *Local:* find maps, businesses, and services in U.S. towns or cities.
- *Language:* get results in different languages.
- *Date:* ask for results in the last three, six, or twelve months.
- *Groups:* discussion groups for online communication.
- *SafeSearch:* filtering to eliminate adult sites from search results.

Alta Vista™ search categories include the *Web, Images, MP3/Audio, Video*, and *News*. You can search worldwide, or just the U.S., and in all languages or English/Spanish. Also included on the home page is *Babel Fish Translation*, where you can translate from/to many languages, whether it is a block of text or an entire Web page.

Directory Search Engines

Directory search engines have the assistance of humans to place Web sites in categories. Rather than searching, they open with a list of categories. Each category has sub-categories. The user works through the categories and eventually is presented with a list of site links.

Arts & Humanities
Photography, History, Literature...

Business & Economy
B2B, Finance, Shopping, Jobs...

Computers & Internet
Software, Web, Blogs, Games...

Education
Colleges, K-12, Distance Learning...

Yahoo® is the most popular and frequently used directory search site on the Web. You can search or browse the directory. A sample of browse categories is shown on the previous page.

Another directory is the *Open Directory Project*. This is the largest human-edited directory on the Web. It was constructed, and is maintained, by a community of volunteers; anyone can contribute by choosing a topic of interest and contributing their expertise by adding, deleting, and updating links. This directory currently contains over five million sites, 590,000 categories, and 70,000 editors.

About.com is another search engine that utilizes people. Here they serve as *Guides to the Internet*. There are over 500 guides that are experts in their field. They offer information and advice, covering over 57,000 topics.

Metasearch Engines

Metasearch engines search other search engines and report the results. These draw from the top search engines, remove duplicate sites, and compile the results.

Dogpile® and *MetaCrawler®* are two metasearch engines that search other search engines, reporting the results by relevance or by the search engine where the sites were found. Both search *Google, MSN®, Yahoo, Ask®*, and more.

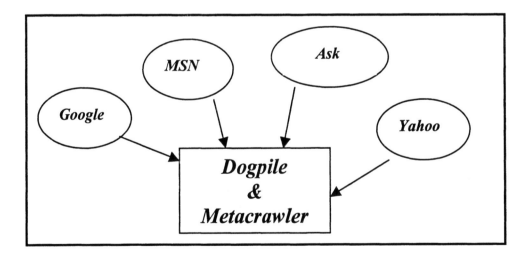

Search Engines for Children

There are specific search engines for children, with searches yielding only *safe* sites. Some of these sites are educational portals, or Web guides, providing much more than a search engine. Often included are sites for specific interests, safe chat rooms, games, activities, sports, news, clubs, and more.

Yahooligans!®, self-named *The Web Guide for Kids*, features a safe search engine for children ages 7-12. Topical areas include *Around the World, Arts & Entertainment, Computers & Games, School Bell, Science & Nature,* and *Sports & Recreation.* Other areas such as news, movies, jokes, games, etc. are also available.

Ask for Kids™ is a search engine where the user asks a question. Sites are identified based on words in the question. The home page includes *Fun & Games, News Resources,* and numerous *Study Tools.*

Two other search engines for children/teens include *KidsClick!*, a directory Web search for kids by librarians, and *Awesome Library for Kids*, a place to search for *School Subjects* or *Fun and More. The Open Directory Project* also has a site for kids and teens.

Search Engine Addresses

About.com	about.com
Alta Vista	www.altavista.com
Ask	www.ask.com
Ask for Kids	www.askforkids.com/
Awesome Library for Kids	www.awesomelibrary.org/student.html
Dogpile	www.dogpile.com
Fast Search	alltheWeb.com
Google	www.google.com
KidsClick	sunsite.berkeley.edu/KidsClick!/
Metacrawler	www.metacrawler.com
Open Directory	dmoz.org
Open Directory – for Kids & Teens	dmoz.org/Kids_and_Teens/
Yahoo	www.yahoo.com

Other Search Engines

The search engines listed above are some of the most common examples from the various categories. There are literally thousands of search engines. *Search Engine Watch* is a Web site that provides information on these and many other search engines. Included are ratings, tutorials, daily and monthly newsletters, and links to search engines in various categories. A sampling of these categories are: *News, Shopping, Multimedia, Kids,* and *Specialty.*

NoodleTools.com is a collection of tools that assist with online research. These tools assist in selecting a search engine, along with citing sources in MLA or APA style. *Choose the Best Search for Your Information Need* is a table that provides links to specific search engines. Look up the information you need, and they identify search engines for that need. This need could be anything from *biographical* to *opinions of current issues* or *primary sources* to *radio programs.*

8.3 - The Invisible Web

The search engines previously identified are part of the "visible Web." This is what you see when doing a Web search, or accessing a subject directory. The "invisible Web" contains information these search engines do not find--they are "invisible" to the searching "spiders." This is not just text, but sounds, images, audio, etc. PDF files are another "find." Spiders are unable to locate these since they are not in HTML format for the Web. There are thousands of specialized databases that cannot be searched by regular search engines. Often, Web pages are generated just for your search; they are not stored anywhere.

An example is searching for books at a university library. When you go to the library's Web site, you can usually search for all of their books from your computer. At the University of Pennsylvania Web site, you can find *The Online Books Page* (onlinebooks.library.upenn.edu). This leads you to over 25,000 free books on the Web. Other databases are available for magazines (www.magportal.com), music, newspapers, museums, etc. The same concept holds true for reference books. Searching for "dinosaurs" will not take you to Encyclopedia Britannica as part of your search. You must go to the Web site of the reference book and perform a search there.

Databases for academic research can be found at *Infomine* (infomine.ucr.edu), *AcademicInfo* (www.academicinfo.net), and *Librarians Internet Index* (lii.org), to name a few. These all have searchable categories, which also take you to academic sites as well as invisible databases. At these sites, as well as regular search engines, searching for terms and including the word "database" in your search will take you to the thousands of invisible Web databases (example: "education database"). *Searchability* (www.searchability.com) provides a list of multi-subject guides (with descriptions) to thousands of search engines covering hundreds of subjects.

When searching for *education database* at *Google*, the first site to appear is ERIC. Introductory text for this site follows:

> *The Education Resources Information Center (ERIC), sponsored by the Institute of Education Sciences (IES) of the U.S. Department of Education, produces the world's premier database of journal and non-journal education literature. The ERIC online system provides the public with a centralized ERIC Web site for searching the ERIC bibliographic database of more than 1.1 million citations going back to 1966. More than 107,000 full-text non-journal documents (issued 1993-2004), previously available through fee-based services only, are now available for free. ERIC is moving forward with its modernization program, and has begun adding materials to the database. [www.eric.ed.gov]*

When using *Advanced Search*, you have the option to choose from publication dates, as well as publication types (shown on the next page).

ERIC Publication Types

Journal Articles	Historical Materials
Book/Product Reviews	Information Analyses
Books	Legal/Legislative/Regulatory Materials
Collected Works - General	Machine-Readable Data Files
Collected Works - Proceedings	Multilingual/Bilingual Materials
Collected Works - Serials	Non-Print Media
Computer Programs	Numerical/Quantitative Data
Creative Works	Opinion Papers
Dissertations/Theses	Reference Materials - Bibliographies
ERIC Digests	Reference Materials - Directories/Catalogs
ERIC Publications	Reference Materials - Vocabularies/Classifications
Guides - Classroom - Learner	Reports - Research
Guides - Classroom - Teacher	Speeches/Meeting Papers
Guides - General	Tests/Questionnaires
Guides - Non-Classroom	Translations

[www.eric.ed.gov/ERICWebPortal/Home.portal?_nfpb=true&_pageLabel=ERIC_Search&Clearme=true]

Another way to access ERIC materials, along with access to *the Gateway to Educational Materials* and other sources, is through the *Educator's Reference Desk*[sm] (www.eduref.org).

> *The Educator's Reference Desk builds on over a quarter century of experience providing high-quality resources and services to the education community. From the Information Institute of Syracuse, the people who created AskERIC, the Gateway to Educational Materials, and the Virtual Reference Desk, the Educator's Reference Desk brings you the resources you have come to depend on. 2,000+ lesson plans, 3,000+ links to online education information, and 200+ question archive responses.* [www.eduref.org]

While many search engines cannot locate *Word, Excel, PDF*, and other non-HTML files, *Gigablast* (www.gigablast.com) locates these, along with files regular search engines can find.

> *Founded in 2000, Gigablast was created to index up to 200 Billion pages with the least amount of hardware possible. Gigablast provides large-scale, high-performance, real-time information retrieval technology for partner sites. The company offers a variety of features including topic generation and the ability to index multiple document formats. This search delivery mechanism gives a partner "turn key" search capability and the capacity to instantly offer search at maximum scalability with minimum cost. In addition, the Gigablast Website (www.gigablast.com) provides unique "Gigabits" of information, enabling visitors to easily refine their search based upon related topics from search results. Clients range from NASDAQ 100 listed corporations to boutique companies.* [www.gigablast.com/about.html]

8.4 - Searching Strategies

Basic Search Engine Procedure

Most search engines operate in much the same way. The search engine has a box where the user enters a key word or words for the topic to be searched. When the search is started, the engine searches the resources of the Web to identify those sources that best match the identified search term(s). The result is the identification of the number of matches found based on the keyword and a ranked list of the sites. For each "hit," the following information is usually provided: (1) the name of the document, (2) a brief description of the document, and (3) a direct link to access the document/site. The most difficult part in the search is choosing the terms to search; sometimes this is a "guessing game."

When accessing the results, it is a good idea to look at the first two or three sites listed. If these (or at least the first ten) are not productive then it is doubtful that the others will be of value. If the results are not productive you can either search again using different words, or use the power search/advanced search feature that most search engines have. This, or a search using Boolean operators such as AND or NOT, might produce more accurate results.

Boolean Searches

Most search tools now use Boolean Logic. That means that if two or more words are identified in the search area (e.g.: math lesson plans), the tool will search for documents with the words grouped in the identified order (math+lesson+plans). Some search engines, however, still search for each of the words separately, resulting in many hits that are not relevant. To be sure that the words are not searched independently, group two or more words together using quotation marks (e.g.: "math lesson plans").

By default, *Google* only returns pages that include all of your search terms. The connector "and" is understood. The order the terms are typed is important.

When searching for "math lesson plans" at *Google*, the following number of pages were returned:

- math lesson plans = 5,820,000
- math + lesson + plans = 5,820,000
- "math lesson plans" = 84, 400
- "lesson plans" + math = 3,170,000
- "math lesson plans" + elementary = 84,100
- "elementary math lesson plans" = 642
- "elementary math lesson plans" + grade 3 = 322
- "algebra lesson plans" = 1,150
- "algebra lesson plans" + advanced = 315
- algebra lesson plans advanced = 815, 000

As you can see, "and" is not necessary, but quotation marks keep the phrase together. Using "+" or "-" also helps to narrow the search. Advanced searches, available as an option in most engines, offer the searcher a variety of options, as explained below. However, when using proper Boolean search logic, the same results occur. When quotes are used, the search is the same as that done in an Advanced Search using "with the exact phrase" option.

Google's Advanced Search Tool helps you locate information quickly by selecting various criteria for your search. You can search for pages:
   • that contain certain words
   • that contain an exact phrase
   • that have at least one of the words you list
   • that contain some words, but without another (same as minus)
   • that are written in a specific language
   • that are in a specific file format
   • that were updated in a specific time frame
   • that have specific terms in various parts of the document
   • that are filtered using *SafeSearch*
   • from a specific site or domain

[Screen from *Google's* Advanced Search]

At the bottom of the page, you can also search for the full text of books and search scholarly pages (along with other features).

✔ **any format**
   Adobe Acrobat PDF (.pdf)
   Adobe Postscript (.ps)
   Microsoft Word (.doc)
   Microsoft Excel (.xls)
   Microsoft Powerpoint (.ppt)
   Rich Text Format (.rtf)

By using the Advanced Search, or adding an extension to any search, you can search for *PDF, Word, Excel, Postscript, PowerPoint,* or *Rich Text Format* documents. These will not appear without this extension used in the search.

8.5 - Filtering Web Searches

It is difficult to supervise every student on the Internet while at school. A question for all schools is whether or not to block access to certain Web sites. Parents are concerned that their children might get into sites where they can view inappropriate or dangerous images. Filters are available, most commonly as software programs, to block undesirable key works, phrases, categories, or sites. Most can be customized by the school for age groups, or to block specific words and categories. Most search engines contain filters as an option so sites can be blocked at home or at school. Filters are not foolproof; students often find ways around them. An alternative is to give students specific Web addresses to go to, or to provide them with bookmarks to use in class, rather than allowing them to "surf the Web." Even if a filter is used, students always need supervision when using the Internet. *Google's SafeSearch* screens for adult sites and eliminates them from search results.

8.6 - The U.S. Government's Official Search Engine

FirstGov.gov is the new and official U.S. gateway to all government information. This search engine transcends the traditional boundaries of government. The vision is global, connecting the world to all U.S. government information and services.

FirstGov.gov
The U.S. Government's Official Web Portal

Placing the Government at your fingertips, this powerful search engine and ever-growing collection of topical and customer-focused links connects you to millions of Web pages ranging from the federal government, local governments, and tribal governments, to foreign nations around the world.

On *FirstGov.gov* you can search millions of Web pages from federal and state governments, the District of Columbia, and U.S. territories. Most of these pages are not available on commercial Websites. FirstGov provides the most comprehensive search of government information anywhere on the Internet.

The site is working with agencies to encourage portals organized around customer groups and topics, instead of agency names. Examples of cross-agency portals include students, people with disabilities, and exporters.

FirstGov.gov also provides a Spanish-language Web portal, *FirstGov en Español*. It is the U.S. government's gateway to thousands of government resources--all in Spanish and developed by, and for, Spanish speakers.

77

8.7 - Activities

• Activity One •

Choose a subject you plan on teaching in the future. (1) Identify a specific topic and grade level. (2) Identify three search terms. (3) Go to three search engines. (4) Perform the same search at each. (5) Reflect on your findings.

• Activity Two •

Choose a research topic you are studying in one of your classes. Using resources from ERIC, search for the topic and report on your findings. (1) Identify the topic you searched. (2) What types of results were obtained? (3) Which components of ERIC were searched? (4) Provide a review of the material you found. If one topic yields poor results, use another topic.

• Activity Three •

Search for lesson plans for a specific topic. Think about the best terms to search. Identify the topic and grade level, the search words, and the number of results found. Do this search three times using similar combinations of words, quotation marks, and Boolean searches techniques. Which search provided the best results? Reflect on your findings.

Tool
9

Teacher and Student Web Sites

9.1 - Introduction

Technology tools have always played an important role in the process of education. In recent years, however, the World Wide Web has surfaced as the preeminent resource tool for teachers. With an initial investment of time and effort to surf the Web, teachers can access and infuse a virtually unlimited number and variety of materials into their teaching. Reference material, teaching strategies, lesson plans, virtual field trips, online projects, puzzles, bulletin board ideas, current events, maps, online exhibits, and worksheets are just a sampling of what the teacher can find on the WWW to use in the classroom.

Just as extensive is the wealth of information and resources available for students. They can look up reference material, practice math problems, search encyclopedias, take interactive quizzes do their homework, and locate primary sources. They may also participate in collaborative projects, virtual field trips, WebQuests, and a myriad of other real time and innovative activities.

The amount of material is so enormous that it would be impossible to discuss all of the possibilities in a single book. This chapter is intended to serve as an introduction to provide guidance for the teacher to begin to explore the multiple resources on the World Wide Web.

9.2 - Educational "Starting Points"

There are a variety of Web sites that are designated as "starting points" for teachers, parents, and students. These often include safe subject resources for students, online projects, curriculum resources for teachers, teaching tips, current events, monthly topics, e-mail, message boards, lesson plans, rubrics, worksheets, and other teacher tools. Some are termed "portals," giving the user a variety of options on the first page. Here, some send teachers, parents, students, or administrators off in different directions to find just what they need. Others are set up as directories of subject resources. Most are totally free, while some have some free resources, as well as those available by subscription. A few sites are by subscription only. A sampling of the most popular (all free resources) are described here.

Kathy Schrock's Guide for Educators (school.discovery.com/schrockguide) is a categorized list of sites useful for enhancing curriculum and professional growth. It is updated often to include the best sites for teaching and learning. This site, now part of *DiscoverySchool.com*, has been the recipient of many awards. Site areas include subject access, search tools, and teacher helpers. The extensive Web links found here are a rich source and excellent starting point for teachers. Access to the many other sites and tools also available from *Discovery School* is provided at this site. One of the best!

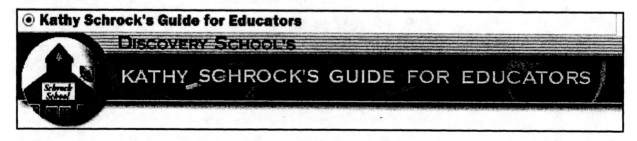

AOL@School® (www.aolatschool.com), available to all, not just AOL subscribers, contains K-12 classroom resources for students, parents, and teachers. Reference materials, tutorials, educational games, and more are available for students. Teachers can find lesson plans, along with classroom resources, tools, and training. For parents, there are resources to assist children with their school work. The home page provides news, monthly features, and learning services. This is an example of a true educational portal.

Education World® (www.educationworld.com) is an excellent site for teachers. Subtitled *The Educator's Best Friend*, this site has six major divisions: *Lesson Planning, Administrator's Desk, School Issues, Professional Development, Technology Integration,* and *Ed. World at Home.* Articles here change often, so check the site daily or weekly. There is a *Joke of the Day, Quote of the Day,* and *Classroom Management Tip of the Day.* Also included are *Article Archives, Subject Resources, Specialties, Reference Center,* and *Featured Programs.* In the *Reference Center* you can subscribe to their newsletters, which will come to you weekly by e-mail. Another weekly feature is *Techtorials,* step-by-step instructions on using some aspect of technology in the regular classroom. These are short, practical, and educationally sound, providing classroom teachers with simple, straightforward tips to use today. An important part of the site contains articles they have published. A search engine takes you to thousands of articles that have been published at *Education World.* Each article also contains links to related sites on the WWW.

Dr. LeBeau's Home Page (www.suelebeau.com) is subtitled "A Resource for Teachers, Students, and Curious Adults." Sue LeBeau, a New Jersey educator, has put together an excellent site for all. Choices on the home page take the user further into additional categories of educational resources for all areas. This site is highly recommended.

Scholastic (www.scholastic.com), known to many for reading resources and books for children, hosts a Web site for Kids, Parents, Teachers, Administrators, and Librarians. *Scholastic News* (for kids) and *BookBeat* are two daily features, along with games, contests, activities, advice, lessons, teacher tools, and more.

Federal Resources for Educational Excellence (FREE) (www.ed.gov/free) provides many free resources for the classroom from the U.S. government. More than 30 federal agencies put hundreds of federally supported teaching and learning resources together to make them easier to find. An easy-to-follow site map guides in your searching.

Teacher Resources at *MarcoPolo* (www.marcopolo-education.org) provides high quality standards-based resources for teachers and students, including Web resources and interactives.

The sites above are examples of the many resources available for teachers. Additional sites can be found at the *15 Highly Effective Instructional Technology Tools* Web site at users.rowan.edu/~levy/15.

9.3 - Lesson Plans

Imagine having a file cabinet containing hundreds of lesson plans. This vision is now a reality. Thousands of teachers have freely shared their lesson plans and teaching ideas by making them available on the Internet as a part of various databases and Web sites. You may not want to use the lesson plan in its entirety; however, online lesson plans can provide ideas, as well as innovative approaches to teaching.

A good starting place is the *Educator's Reference Desk* (www.eduref.org). This combines resources from *AskERIC*, the *Gateway to Educational Materials*, and the *Virtual Reference Desk*. There are over 2,000 lesson plans, 3,000 links to online education information, and 200 question archive responses at this site. Lesson plans can be browsed by subject, or you can search their database by topic and grade level.

Search the Lesson Plan Collection

Describe what you are looking for. Searching Tips.

should contain ▼	the words ▼	all fields ▼

☐ Pre-K	☐ 1st	☐ 2nd	☐ 3rd	☐ 4th	☐ 5th	☐ 6th
☐ Kinder.	☐ 7th	☐ 8th	☐ 9th	☐ 10th	☐ 11th	☐ 12th

There are many other sources of lesson plans on the Web (a few are shown below; see the *Technology Tools for Teachers* Web site for a more complete listing). Other sites can be found through searches. Unfortunately, there is no easy way to search all of the databases and instantly find just what you need. Look through some of the choices and bookmark those that have possibilities for your subject/grade level.

Education World's Lesson Planning Center (www.education-world.com/a_lesson) features new lesson plans (they publish a new lesson plan daily), along with other archives by subject area. Current lessons, lesson plan articles, and lesson planning resources are featured here.

The Lesson Plans Page (www.lessonplanspage.com) houses over 2,500 lesson plans. Choose your subject from the categories: *math, science, music, language arts, computers & Internet, social studies, art, PE & health, other,* and *multi-disciplinary.*

N.Y. Times Teacher Connections (www.nytimes.com/learning/teachers), for grades 6–12, provides daily lesson plans, lesson plan archives, news, puzzles, and more.

PBS Teacher Source (www.pbs.org/teachersource) features over 3,000 lesson plans and activities. A search engine is available, or you can browse by subject.

9.4 - Teacher Utilities

Every teacher can use help in the classroom with daily tasks such as grading; making out tests; and producing rubrics, worksheets, puzzles, certificates, and other handouts. Software can be purchased for these tasks; however, it is possible you might find some free utilities available on the WWW. As with some of the other sites, some of the utilities are free for teachers, while others have a fee involved. Some companies also offer free trials of their software for the teacher to use, evaluate, and compare the various products. To find those currently available, it is best to do a search, as availability of utilities on the WWW changes frequently.

Puzzles

There are a number of free puzzle-making utilities on the WWW that can be used by both teachers and students.

PuzzleMaker is available as a free resource at *Discovery School's* site (www.puzzlemaker.com). Options include *Fallen Phrases, Letter Tiles, Cryptograms, Double Puzzle, Math Square, Number Blocks, Word Search, Criss-Cross Puzzle, Hidden Message*, and *Mazes*.

At *Crossword Puzzle Games* (www.crosswordpuzzlegames.com), you can create you own crosswords, or do theirs.

FunBrain's Word Turtle (www.funbrain.com/detect/) is a seek-and-find word search game. Enter a list of words, and they are hidden in a puzzle. Levels can be selected. Children can play against *FunBrain*, or print the puzzle out on paper.

Other Utilities

Bulletin board ideas are available from *Discovery School, Kathy Schrock's Guide for Educators*, and *Education World*, along with many other sites. Just search for "bulletin board" + the topic you need. *Learning Page* (www.learningpage.com) and *ABC Teach*® (www.abcteach.com) are two excellent sites for worksheets. *RubiStar* (rubistar.4teachers.org/index.php) is a free tool to help teachers create rubrics. They can save and edit them for a year on *RubiStar's* site. *Web Workshop Wizard* (wizard.4teachers.org) is one of several online tools found at *4Teachers.org*. This permits teachers to create worksheets, lessons, and Web pages and post them on the Web.

Sue LeBeau has compiled a long listing (www.suelebeau.com/freetools.htm) of free tools for teachers on her site. These include quiz generators, worksheets, flashcards, games, puzzles, certificates, forms, calendars, templates, and more.

Remember, when you find good utilities, as well as other sites, bookmark them for future use. You might even want to begin a notebook of teaching resources, lesson plans, and ideas you find for classroom use.

9.5 - Sites for New Teachers

As a pre-service teacher and a new teacher, you need basic information about being in a new classroom and being a new teacher. Below are descriptions of some sites to assist you. Links to these sites are on the *Technology Tools for Teachers* Web site. There you will also find a number of articles for new teachers from *Education World*, along with other sites for the new teacher.

Scholastic-Resources for New and Future Teachers: resources and advice for new teachers. At the top of the page are links to the main Scholastic site, along with *Online Activities, Lesson Plans,* and *Tools.*

NEA Works 4 Me Tips Library: an archive for *NEA's Weekly Classroom Tips* e-mail. This library contains more than 400 tips offering ideas and solutions that you can use in your classroom.

New Teacher Resources: resources from *TeachersFirst*, a Web resource for K-12 classroom teachers who want useful resources and lesson plans to use with their students.

A New Teacher's Survival Guide: a guidebook; substitutes for a mentor when you need help.

Survival Guide for New Teachers: an online book from the U.S. Department of Education. This is a guide to how new teachers can work effectively with veteran teachers, parents, principals, and teacher educators.

Online Resources for New Teachers: part of a course designed for new teachers at the Oswego City School District, this site can help you by providing you with one-stop shopping for many of the resources that you will find beneficial.

Ideas for New Teachers and Education Students: information ranging from lesson planning and writing behavioral objectives to ideas about classroom management and descriptions of the advantages and disadvantages of different instructional methods. Click on the home page for more categories.

NEA-Helping New Teachers Survive and Thrive: a guide for NEA local affiliates interested in creating new teacher support systems.

The First Days of Middle School: help for new teachers, the first days of school, discipline, and classroom management are the main categories of this site.

Beginning Teachers' Tool Box: while part is an advertisement for a book they publish, the section, *New Teacher's Home Page*, contains good practical tips and resources.

Teacher Resource Center: from the Georgia Department of Education – links to many documents for the first-year teacher.

9.6 - Online Projects

Collaboratively or individually, students can participate in a variety of projects and activities that are posted on the WWW. Collaborative, online projects are one of the most exciting ways to motivate students. Students get involved by posting projects on the Web, e-mailing other students or experts, discussing issues on a threaded discussion, or holding an online chat.

Most collaborative learning projects are placed on the Web at nationally acclaimed sites housing online projects. These projects are for students to collaborate not just with their classmates, but with students around the world. Through these experiences, students learn to use the Web to engage in data exchanges with students from other schools, collaborate on writing projects, and participate in world expeditions and explorations. Most sites and experiences are free; however, some require a registration fee. A few of the most popular are described below.

The *Global Schoolhouse* (www.gsn.org) hosts a variety of collaborative projects each year. The original clearinghouse for collaborative projects, this not-for-profit organization has been linking classrooms around the world since 1984. Free membership provides project-based learning support materials, resources, activities, lessons, and special offers to schools. Over 90,000 educators in over 194 countries now collaborate on projects. Future, current, and archived projects can be accessed on their Web site.

JASON Project (www.jasonproject.org) was founded in 1989. Its mission is to inspire in students a life-long passion for learning in science, math, and technology through hands-on, real-world scientific discovery. It gives educators exciting new ways to teach standards-based mathematics and provides students with hands-on approaches to solving real scientific problems while gaining technology-rich learning experiences.

ThinkQuest (www.thinkquest.org), sponsored by the Oracle Education Foundation, is "all about students thinking and learning together." Working in teams, students compete to create the "best educational Web sites," while they also compete for exciting prizes, including a trip to *ThinkQuest Live*, an educational extravaganza celebrating their achievements. The teams' Web sites are published for the world to see in the *ThinkQuest Library*. This rich online resource contains over 5,500 educational Web sites, created by students for students. You can search the library to find many intriguing sites.

Journey North (www.learner.org/jnorth), from Annenberg Media, engages students in a global study of wildlife migration and seasonal change. K-12 students share their own field observations with classmates across North America. They track the coming of spring through the migration patterns of monarch butterflies, bald eagles, robins, hummingbirds, whooping cranes, and other birds and mammals; the budding of plants; changing sunlight; and other natural events. Standards-based lesson plans, activities, and information help students make local observations and fit them into a global context.

9.7 - Virtual Field Trips

Virtual Field trips can be taken to places impossible to visit without the Web. Real-life pictures and movies can bring the sites to life. These electronic trips are a way to integrate the Internet into the curriculum by allowing students to "visit" places being studied. Visits can be made to the Smithsonian Institute, the White House, the Louvre in Paris, or the Metropolitan Museum of Art in New York, along with thousands of other places just by entering a Web address.

When having students take virtual field trips, make it clear to them why they are doing this. Give them an assignment or project to do while traveling, such as taking the trip in groups, with resources to locate along the way.

Searching the WWW is one way to locate these trips. Another way is to visit Web sites developed for this purpose.

The *Virtual Tours* site (www.virtualfreesites.com/tours.html) is a good place to start. This is a collection of over 500 tours of the world, museums, exhibits, points of special interest, and the U.S. government. The site's goal is to provide information that will enhance any Internet journey. Included are over 300 museums, exhibits, and points of interest. Many of these offer

multimedia guided tours, including text, pictures, sounds, and movies. Cities and countries can also be visited through interactive journeys. Also included here is travel related information, including traveling tips, world maps, health information, brochures, weather forecasts, restaurant guides, hostels, and more. The government section includes the White House, branches of the U.S. government, House and Senate Web sites, Library of Congress exhibits, historical documents, and much more.

Utah Education Network (www.uen.org/utahlink/tours) also hosts a virtual field trip site. Their field trips are all geared to the classroom and categorized by subjects. Some of these include: *Fine Arts, Foreign Language, Health/PE, Language Arts, Math, Science, Social Studies,* and *Special Ed.* You can visit violin makers, discover artists and their work, take a European vacation, or a journey through the digestive system. Another part of the site provides directions for the teacher to create their own field trip.

Apple Learning Interchange (ali.apple.com/ali_sites/ali/new_events.html) hosts a number of *Digital Learning Events.* They have virtual field trips to dinosaur digs, the Grand Canyon, or a trip through the history of women's baseball. Your students can also tour *Lewis and Clark Then and Now,* featuring Webcasts, videoconferencing, and movie clips from an extensive recreation of their expedition. This site also has content experts to bring to the classroom through Webcasts and video and audio interviews.

Investigate these trips; then read about WebQuests, another form of online projects, in the next chapter. You will see how Internet resources can turn your classroom into an exciting and rewarding learning experience.

9.8 - Student Homework, Reference, and Resource Sites

The WWW is a powerful tool to help with daily homework. It can also assist in locating reference material and resources for projects. Some sites are specifically for reference, while others are divided into subject areas for homework, project resources, and just plain fun.

Homework Helper Sites

B.J. Pinchbeck's Homework Helper (school.discovery.com/homeworkhelp/bjpinchbeck) is a good place to start for homework and reference assistance. Now hosted by *Discovery School*, this site has links for doing homework in any area, along with a *Reference* section featuring over 100 reference books available on the Internet. Homework links include *Art/Music, Computer Science & Internet, English, Foreign Languages, Health & P.E., Math, Science,* and *Social Studies*. Also included are *News, Recess, Reference,* and *Search Engines*. Lots of excellent resource and reference sites can be found here.

Homework Spot™ (www.homeworkspot.com) is a one-site-has-all place to visit. Subject listings are available for Elementary, Middle, and High School. Also included are menus with links to Reference and Current Events sites. Areas include *Must See Sites, To Do, Field Trips, Exhibits, You Asked For It,* etc. *Must Sees* include B.J. Pinchbeck's (above). Featured encyclopedias are *Britannica.com, Encyclopedia.com,* and *Encarta.com*.

Reference Desk
Almanacs
Ask an Expert
Atlases
Biographies
Calculators
Calendars
Citations
Current Events
Dictionaries
Encyclopedias
Government
Homework Hotlines
Libraries
Lists
Museums
People
Reading Room
Q&A
Quotations
Safe search engines
Statistics
Thesauri
Trivia
Much More...

Subject levels include *Homeroom, Arts & Crafts, Fine Arts, English, Language Art, Foreign Languages, Health/Fitness, Math, Science, Social Studies, Technology,* and more.

MUST-SEE SITES
The Internet Public Library
B.J. Pinchbeck's
Multnomah Homework Center
LibrarySpot.com

Refdesk.com's Homework Helper (www.refdesk.com/homework.html) provides links for grade levels and a *Homework Center* link. This takes the student to Multnomah County Library where they can receive *Live Homework Help* and access a variety of Homework topics. *Refdesk* also provides a listing of Other Homework Links and Tools for Research. Links are available to go to the main *Refdesk* and access *Ask the Experts, Quick Reference/Research,* and *Facts Subject Index.*

Reference Sites

Refdesk (www.refdesk.com), included above as a Homework Helper site, is not just for homework (or kids). It is a comprehensive reference site, with the homework area being only a small part. Some of the site's major areas include *Search Resources, Headlines, Today's Pictures, Daily Diversions, Weather, Breaking News, Potpourri, Reference Resources, Facts Search Desk, Subject Categories,* and *Just for Fun.* A sampling of topics in these areas, helpful to students, appear in the chart below. Their motto says it all: "The single best source for facts on the Net." The best!

Acronyms	Calendars	Grammar/Style	Quotations
Almanacs	Countries	Maps	States
Ask the Experts	Dictionaries	Medical	Thesaurus
Biographies	Encyclopedias	Newspapers	White/Yellow Pages
Calculators	Government	People	Zip/Area Codes

The Internet Public Library (www.ipl.org) contains a variety of subject collections, reference materials, and a Reading Room. Also at the IPL is *KidsSpace @ The Internet Public Library* (www.ipl.org/youth) featuring a Reference area, and an area for Teachers & Parents. *Reference* includes *The World, Computers/Internet, Health & Nutrition, Reading Zone, Math & Science, Art & Music, Sports & Recreation,* and *Fun Stuff.* Each category takes you to topics, each linking to many appropriate Web sites. There is also a link to *TeenSpace,* the *Internet Public Library for Teens.*

Fact Monster™ (www.factmonster.com) from *Information Please*© features an online almanac, dictionary, encyclopedia, and homework help. Areas cover the *World, United States, People, Sports, Science, Math & Money, Word Wise, Arts & Living,* and *Games & Quizzes.* A search engine is also included.

For additional reference work, there are several encyclopedias online. *Encarta*® *Encyclopedia* (encarta.msn.com/artcenter_/browse.html) contains over 4,500 articles, sidebars, literature guides, archives, and homework starters. *Encyclopedia Britannica Online* is also available (www.britannica.com). Searches take you not only to articles in the encyclopedia, but to other references on the WWW. The articles in Britannica include hyperlinks to other articles, photos, and multimedia. Articles are printable and can be e-mailed to others.

Additional dictionaries, almanacs, thesauruses, etc. can be found at *RefDesk, BJ Pinchbeck's Homework Helper,* or through searches.

Primary Sources

Original text, research or writings on a subject, or records of events described or recorded by a participant or witness are considered to be primary sources. These may include letters, manuscripts, diaries, journals, newspapers, speeches, interviews, government documents, recordings, etc. These sources serve as raw material to interpret the past; often combined with other interpretations by historians, they provide resources for historical research. Excellent information on finding primary resources can be found in the history section at the American Library Association (www.lib.washington.edu/subject/History/RUSA).

The *Library of Congress* (www.loc.gov) is the best place to find primary sources. Manuscripts, maps, films, audio recordings, prints, photographs, and music can all be found at this site. With more than ten million primary sources online, there is something for everyone. Teachers can also visit *The Learning Page* for lesson plans and activities using primary sources.

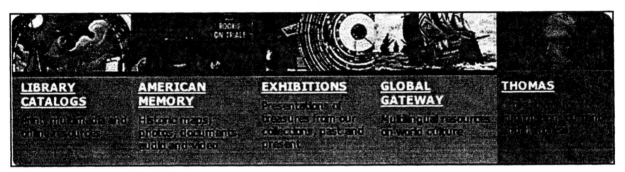

Resource and Fun Sites

Alfy (www.alfy.com), "the Web portal for kids," is geared toward children 3-9 years old. Developed so children this age can safely and easily use the Web, *Alfy* is fun as well as educational. It is stocked with interactive stories, games, crafts, activities, and more. Eight centers entertain and educate children: *Brain Train* (the toddler place), *Music Mania* (play, record, and listen to music), *Storyville* (interactive stories), *Create!* (art studio), *Clubhouse* (communicate with others), *Surprises* (jokes and riddles), *Alfy's Arcade* (game center), and *Alfy's Cool Sites* (gateway to the Internet).

Berit's Best Sites for Children (www.beritsbest.com) provides links to the 1,000 best sites for children. All sites are categorized in topical areas. The home page also includes the 25 best sites chosen by visitors and a search engine for the site.

FunBrain.com™ (www.funbrain.com) is for kids in grades K-8 and teachers. Full of interactive educational resources, quizzes, and games, *FunBrain* is educational as well as fun. *Curriculum Guides* and *Standards Finder* help teachers choose the appropriate games and activities for their students. They can even print out flash cards.

4Kids.org (www.4kids.org) is "your link to the latest tecKNOWLEDGEy on the Web." Here you can find an assortment of safe Web sites, games, and fun for children.

9.9 - Activities

• Activity One •

Identify a unit and grade level you will be teaching. Visit four of the educational "Starting Points" listed to find resources available to teach the unit. At each site locate reference material for the unit and an activity to use in the unit. For each site, provide: (1) An overview of what you found at the site. (2) A description of the specific reference material and activity for your unit. (3) The Web address for both the reference material and activity.

• Activity Two •

Identify a unit and grade level you will be teaching. Visit four sites with lesson plans, either those identified, or others you find through searches. Choose the four best lesson plans you find for your unit. For each, provide: (1) The name of the lesson plan. (2) The site where you found it. (3) The Web address for the lesson plan. (4) A brief description of the lesson.

• Activity Three •

Identify a unit and grade level you will be teaching. Using vocabulary for that unit, construct a puzzle at one of the identified Web sites. Use a minimum of ten words and definitions in the puzzle. Print out the puzzle and the answers.

• Activity Four •

Identify a unit and grade level you will be teaching. Visit three sites for online projects and/or virtual field trips. Describe three projects (with the Web address) you feel would be useful in your classroom (50 words minimum for each project).

• Activity Five •

Visit the Library of Congress. Go to *Teachers–The Learning Page–Features & Activities*. Choose one activity. Write a reflection (minimum 100 words) about this feature/activity and how it would be an effective teaching resource.

• Activity Six •

Be a kid! Using the Resource and Fun Sites, find two educational games/activities you enjoy. Describe each, including how it could be used in the classroom (minimum 50 words each).

Tool
10

Scavenger Hunts and WebQuests

10.1 - Introduction

Students spend a lot of time on the Internet, with many students using it primarily for e-mail, instant messaging, or games. Teaching students to search properly is one way to assist them in finding what they need for their education, but they must also learn to do something with what they find. Web-based learning activities can help you teach your students to do this. These activities have the potential to enhance learning, while making it exciting to the students. One simple activity is to create scavenger hunts for students.

More sophisticated Web-based learning activities have students do something with what they locate on the Internet. They should be able to determine its meaning, compile and synthesize various sources, and critique the usefulness of the material. Most projects of this type are not just to locate factual information, but also to take it a step further and utilize higher-level thinking skills when synthesizing the information. The most popular form of this type of Web-based learning activity is the WebQuest.

Once these activities have been created, it is helpful to have them published on a Web site for easy student access. *Filamentality* is a Web site for teachers to assist in creating these, and other Web-based activities. Teachers can go there to create five different types of activities, which can then be posted for free on *Filamentality's* Web site.

10.2 - Scavenger Hunts

Scavenger hunts, also called treasure hunts, provide students with a fun way to search the Internet, improve reading skills, improve comprehension skills, and practice problem solving. They are easy for the teacher, or even the student, to create. Hunts can be used in any subject area, at any grade level; whereby students learn more about a topic, along with technology at the same time. Individuals, or groups of students, can work on the scavenger hunt. It can be as simple or involved as the teacher wants it to be. While there are different types, all can be developed to be informative and generate knowledge of the subject.

Teachers often find Web pages, with a wealth of educational information on them, useful in a subject they teach. It would be boring for a student to just go and read the material. The teacher can gather a collection of Web pages (specific ones, not the entire site), then pose one or more questions for the student to answer using each Web page. In searching for the specific answer, the student is exposed to photos, videos, and other factual material on the identified page. Questions can get more difficult, having students synthesize what they have learned on other pages. A synthesizing question, needing good comprehension of the subject, can be placed at the end to pull all of their thoughts and research together.

This is one type of scavenger hunt that, along with other types, is illustrated on the following pages.

Sample Scavenger Hunts

The sample scavenger hunts illustrated here use the theme: *History of Rowan University*. The activity is intended to acquaint a Rowan student with some significant events that have happened at this institution in the past.

Each scavenger hunt will utilize the same Web sites and information, but show how you can construct various types of scavenger hunts for your students.

1. **Teaching Searching Skills**
   (disadvantage: students can "roam" the Web without supervision)

   Directions: Search the Web to find facts about Rowan University. Use *Google* to search for answers to the following questions. Provide the answer, along with the site where you found the answer.

Fact to Search	Answer	Web Site Where Found
Two other names for Rowan University before its current name.		
The year the institution was established.		
An event that occurred in 1967 to put the college "in the news."		
The name of the building where this event occurred.		
The year Rowan University got this name. Why did this change take place?		
Who is Robert Hegyes and how is he affiliated with Rowan?		

2. Searching One Web Site
(advantage: cannot "roam" the Internet; disadvantage: limited information)

Directions: go to the Web site below; find answers to the questions listed.
http://www.rowan.edu/subpages/about/history/

1. _____ What was the mission of the institution when it was established?

2. _____ When was the institution established?

3. _____ How much money was donated by Henry and Betty Rowan?

4. _____ When and how did the institution get worldwide attention?

5. _____ Who is the current president of Rowan University?

6. _____ How long has he been president at Rowan?

3. Search at Specific Web Sites
(advantages: cannot "roam" the Internet; more sites to search and read)

Directions: Use only the sites below to find the relevant information and answers to questions. (Web sites could be hyperlinks on a Web page for easy access. Another way to do this would be to have a specific Web site for each question.)

Glassboro's History:
http://www.glassboroonline.com/history_glassboro.html

The History of Rowan University:
http://www.rowan.edu/subpages/about/history/

The Historic Private Gift:
http://rowanmagazine.com/features/feature5/

Wikipedia, the Free Encyclopedia:
http://en.wikipedia.org/wiki/Rowan_University

1. In the early years, Rowan gained a national reputation in what educational areas?

2. Give all names the university has had, and in what years the names changed.

3. List three areas of interest to you on Rowan University's Web site.

4. Briefly describe the conference held at Hollybush in 1967.

5. Provide the names of three individuals who have been instrumental in the growth of Rowan University.

6. Explain Henry Rowan's background and how/why that is important to the future of Rowan University.

4. Other types of Scavenger Hunts

Another type that could be used, but not applicable for this scavenger hunt topic, would be to make a list of questions, each pertaining to a specific person, place, etc. Provide another list of Web sites for each person or place. The student must read each site to match the answer about the person/place with that person/place. Other examples can include text and photos on a Web site, along with questions and hyperlinks to the sites where additional information can be found; or, place links in sentences about the topics.

10.3 - WebQuests

WebQuests are inquiry-oriented activities in which students interact with resources on the Internet. They have proven to be a safe and educationally sound way for teachers to take full advantage of the multitude of resources available on the Internet. WebQuests can be short, lasting for only one or two periods, or longer, where the student searches for and analyzes larger bodies of information. WebQuests are often group activities that assign a different role to each member of the group, and are often interdisciplinary, covering several subjects.

Students learn about their WebQuest through an introduction. This explains the project and often provides background information. They are then given a task that is accomplished by searching a set of resources. Most of these are teacher-identified sites found on the Internet (with hyperlinks in the instructions). Other non-Internet references can be provided by the teacher. Students are also provided with instructions and assistance on how to carry out the WebQuest. Fact-finding is not the only activity. As students analyze the variety of teacher-specified resources, they use critical thinking skills to solve the identified problem.

WebQuests were developed by Bernie Dodge at San Diego State University in 1995 as a way for teachers to integrate the power of the Internet with student learning. Tom March later worked with him on the project. They continue to do research in the area and make materials available for teachers. Bernie Dodge hosts *The WebQuest Page* (Webquest.sdsu.edu), while *Ozline.com* (www.ozline.com/learning/) is the home of Tom March's educational initiatives. Both of these should be visited for sample WebQuests, assistance on developing WebQuests, and ideas for classroom implementation. The information in this unit is based on their model.

Learning about WebQuests

Teachers can create their own WebQuests or take advantage of the many WebQuests available on the Internet. Many of these have been developed by students in classes taught by Dodge and March, while others have been developed by teachers who have adopted their model.

One place to learn about WebQuests is to look at the training materials on Dodge's WebQuest page (Webquest.sdsu.edu/materials.htm). A good way to begin is to participate in *A WebQuest about WebQuests* for your grade level. Each level provides five WebQuests and has teachers examine each from different points of view:

- the Efficiency Expert (values time in the classroom);
- the Affiliator (the best activities are when students work together);
- the Altitudinist (a proponent of higher level thinking); and
- the Technophile (the WebQuest makes the best use of the technology of the Web).

After completing this WebQuest, investigate other sample WebQuests on the Internet. Dodge's *The WebQuest Page* is a good place to start. Go to webquest.org; on the left of this page click on *Find WebQuests*. There you will find a search engine for various subjects and grades. Tom March's site featuring WebQuests is *Best WebQuests* (www.bestWebquests.com). *Blue Web'n* also has a number of WebQuests (www.blueWebn.com); search for "Webquests." A few sample topics from these sites are below:

- Poetry Quest
- Weather WebQuest
- Culture Quest
- Smoking Is Cool ... Not!
- Art Exhibit
- The Art of Mathematics
- Staff Development WebQuest
- Should Schools Filter Web Content?
- Animals of the Rainforest
- Trip to Germany
- Museum Mischief
- Math and Stocks
- Women in Science
- Diary of Anne Frank
- The Internet for Teachers
- Ancient Olympic Games

As seen from the titles above, WebQuests can be on any topic, and for any grade level. They could be used to analyze a contemporary problem, or be the basis for role playing a figure in history. Products of WebQuests can be a written or oral report, a multimedia project, a display, artwork, or even a performance. The ideas are endless.

Prior to developing a WebQuest, the teacher should have a clear and detailed answer to the following questions:

- What do I want the students to learn?
- How will the students be motivated to learn?
- What resources are necessary?
- How will I assess students' learning?

Developing a WebQuest

Bernie Dodge has developed six **Building Blocks of a WebQuest**. These should all be included in a WebQuest. Often *Process* and *Resources* are combined, as resources are considered a part of the process.

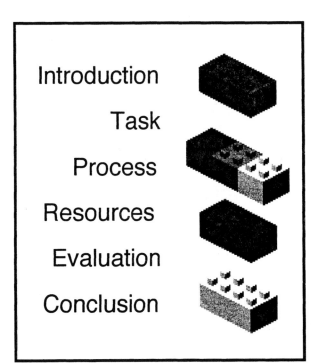

In the *Introduction*, the student is oriented to what will be taking place. It is the time to create interest in the project by emphasizing the relevance and importance of the WebQuest to the student and to making the WebQuest fun and interesting for the student.

The *Task* is the most important part of a WebQuest, as it provides goals and focus to the project. What are the students expected to learn? How will they accomplish this? Explain to them what will take place and the sequence of what they will do. What will be the final outcome of the WebQuest?

The *Process* includes the steps the students are to follow to accomplish the task. Provide a description of each student's role and their responsibilities in that role. How should they organize the facts they find; what do they do with them? *Resources* include hyperlinks to all Web pages the students are to use, along with additional resources they might use. These could include videos, library resources, textbooks, etc. *Evaluation*, often in the form of a rubric, measures the effectiveness of the WebQuest as a learning activity. The *Conclusion* summarizes the experience and reflects upon what was learned.

To understand these Building Blocks better, go to Dodge's Training Materials and go to *Building Blocks for WebQuests* (projects.edtech.sandi.net/staffdev/buildingblocks/p-index.htm). Here each section essential to any WebQuest is described, with examples of WebQuests for each section.

Evaluating WebQuests

Teachers can develop their own evaluation tools to evaluate their own WebQuest. Dodge and March both have rubrics on their sites to help you be sure the WebQuest you create is doing all it should do.

Dodge's can be found at: edWeb.sdsu.edu/Webquest/Webquestrubric.html
March's can be found at: bestwebquests.com/bwq/matrix.asp

Below are some of the characteristics of a well-developed WebQuest (in an abbreviated form):

Overall Visual Appeal	Appealing graphic elements are included; differences in fonts, colors.
Effectiveness of Introduction	The Introduction draws the reader into the lesson by relating to learner's interests or setting up a problem; builds on learner's prior knowledge.
Cognitive Level of the Task	Task requires synthesis of many resources, and/or going beyond the data given and making a generalization or product.
Technical Sophistication of the Task	Task requires use of multimedia software, video, conferencing.
Clarity and Richness of Process	Each step is clear; students always know where they are in the project; there are a variety of activities, roles, and perspectives.
Quantity and Quality of Resources	Many resources are provided on the Internet and in the classroom; links make good use of Web resources.
Clarity of Evaluation Criteria	Criteria for gradations of success are stated; often in the form of a rubric for self, peer, or teacher use.

10.4 - Publishing on the WWW

Simple WebQuests, and other Web-based activities, can be created in a *Word* document. Most, however, are developed as Web pages, as seen in examples on the Internet. To do this, you will need Web development software and a location to host your page. *DreamWeaver*® and *Front Page*® are two common Web development packages, but they do take a long time to learn and are expensive. You can also use *Netscape* (versions 7.2 or older) that includes *Netscape Composer*, for a free, easy to use Web development program.

Filamentality

Filamentality is an online publishing tool that will let you create online learning activities and post them for free at their site. Originally developed by Tom March in 1996, *Filamentality* now resides on a site that is sponsored by AT & T Education (www.kn.sbc.com/wired/fil/). The name was developed because the site helps the teacher combine the <u>fil</u>aments of the Web with a learner's <u>mentality</u>.

Filamentality helps a teacher create five types of online activity formats:

> *Hotlist:* A list of sites (hyperlinks) for students to access on a Web page. Resources for a unit can be combined and posted for easy access by students. Students can also use this to publish findings of their research.

> *Multimedia Scrapbook:* Sites are organized into categories for easy use; text is incorporated to provide instructions for students or add information about the sites. Students can download items for use in projects, reports, or their own scrapbook.

> *Subject Sampler:* Students are provided with several interesting and interactive Web sites on a particular topic. These sites provide "something for the student to do"; not just read factual information. Students are asked to carry out several of the activities and respond about the activities from a personal perspective.

> *Treasure Hunt:* Similar to scavenger hunts, (earlier in this chapter), the teacher finds 10-15 Web sites and constructs a question the students must find on each. It can be used to learn facts, to assist in reading for a purpose, or to review a unit.

> *WebQuest:* A way to put a WebQuest the teacher develops on a free Web page for students to access.

Filamentality guides you as you develop a topic, search the Web for resources, and use their fill-in-the-blank tool to make your own online learning activities.

Tom March also developed *Web 'n Flow* ($25 per year). This allows teachers to design Web activities for their students and post them on a Web site. More powerful than *Filamentality*, it includes activity formats and evaluation rubrics. Schools' Web sites can be powered by *Web 'n Flow*, and activities created by the teachers can appear in a matrix on the school Web site. Bernie Dodge has a new program: *QuestGarden* ($20 per year). This is also an authoring tool and hosting site for WebQuests. *QuestGarden* helps the teacher set up a WebQuest with the sections discussed earlier in this chapter.

10.5 - Activities

• Activity One •

Design a scavenger hunt as part of a lesson you are developing. Use one of the models in this chapter. Have 15 items in your "hunt." Create a word-processed handout for your students. On a separate sheet of paper, include the answers.

• Activity Two •

Design a WebQuest that will be part of a unit you are developing. Remember, this is not a scavenger hunt where your students just look for facts. This can be developed as a *Word* document. Web addresses will change to hyperlinks when the Return/Enter key is "hit." Include a few pieces of clip art, but keep it simple.

- Include the six "Building Blocks" in your project; you may combine Process and Resources.
- Plan to have students work in groups of three or four, with each student having a different "job."
- Include at least six Web links for the students to use.
- When you think you have your WebQuest finished, use Tom March's rubric to see if you have covered all areas.
- It is not necessary to create a rubric for grading your students.

Prior to developing your WebQuest:

- Go to webquest.org; search for similar subjects and grades. Look at three WebQuests for similar topics.
- In Bernie Dodge's Training Materials, look at *Building Blocks for WebQuests*.

• Activity Three •

Use *Filamentality* to create a "Hotlist" for a lesson you are developing. Include it as a resource with your lesson plan.

Tool

11

Web Pages

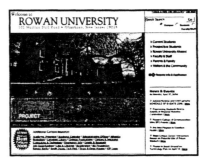

11.1 - Introduction

You (or your students) can design a Web site for your class, your school, your organization, or your family. Having a Web site establishes YOU on the World Wide Web. It is not a difficult task, but in the beginning it can be a bit time consuming. The end result will be worth the effort. Simple, easy-to-follow instructions in this chapter will help you along.

Where do you begin?

- There are sites on the Internet that allow teachers and students to create and post classroom Web pages using a template that is provided on their site.
- Simple, free, Web authoring programs, such as *Netscape Composer* (a component of *Netscape Communicator*), are available on the Web to let the user create simple Web pages.
- Some word processing programs (*Microsoft Word, AppleWorks*®) allow text to be saved as HTML, bypassing the use of a Web authoring program.
- For the advanced user with more complex pages, programs like *Dreamweaver* (Macromedia) and *Frontpage* (Microsoft) are available for purchase (tutorials can be found on the Web for these).

In this chapter, you will learn how to do all of the above, with the exception of the advanced programs. As mentioned above, pages constructed on sites for teachers/students, are published on these respective sites. For others, you must have a place to publish your Web page.

11.2 - Getting Started

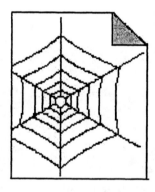

- A Web site is composed of any number of pages; the first page is called the "home page."
- Each page is supported with links to other places on the Internet, images, sounds, or movies.
- It is no longer necessary to be a programmer, or know HTML (Hypertext Markup Language), to construct a Web site.
- The user manipulates the objects, while the program inserts the code as needed.
- Web authoring programs allow the user to place text and graphics on the page, format and reposition the text and graphics, and make links to other sites on the Internet and places within the site being created.

If your students can make Web pages, so can you!

Components of a Web Page

The major components of a Web page are similar in all Web authoring programs:

- Header (similar to the headline in a newspaper)
- Background color, pattern, or texture
- Text: fonts, sizes, and colors
- Images: graphics, photos, sounds, movies
- Links: text or graphics that get the user to another page from the home page, or to other Internet sites
- Tables: easy ways to organize components in rows and columns (divisions do not have to show)
- Horizontal rules: break the page into horizontal divisions

How to Create a Web Site

This section contains generic tips for designing and constructing a Web site. Instructions for authoring programs follow.

Designing a Web Site

1. Plan and organize
   Prior to actually creating a Web site on the computer, it is essential to develop an outline, or storyboard, for the project. (Look at other Web pages for ideas.) First, determine the focus of your site. Then plan and sketch out the tentative layout for each page. Don't make the site too complex. Sites can be linear, hierarchical, or in a Webbed design (links going to many locations). Regardless of the format you use, always include links to get back to the home page.

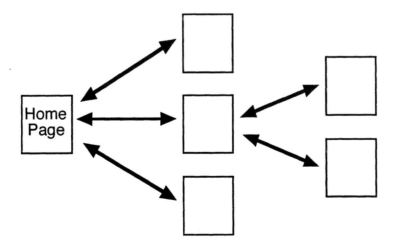

2. Gather images, links, etc.
   While in the planning process, find clip art, photos, or other graphics to be used, and determine links to other Web pages that will be needed.

3. Compose each page

    Remember this site will be viewed by others; organization and simplicity are of the utmost importance. In addition, each page should be built around a theme or topic, be attractive and easy to navigate, and be linked back to the home page.

4. Enter and format text

    Text can be entered directly onto the Web page or pasted from a word processing document (be careful, it might not appear as it did in the original document). Various sizes for headings and text are available. Text styles, colors, and alignments can also be applied.

5. Add images

    Images can be digital photos, clip art from CDs, original art, scanned photos, or clip art from the Internet. All must be in *.gif* or *.jpeg* formats. *QuickTime* movies can also be imported into pages. (The larger the images are, the longer it will take the page to load; and the more space it will take to save the page.) Save all components in the same folder as the Web pages.

6. Add links

    Links are of two types: those that take the user somewhere else in the Web site and those that link to another Web site on the Internet. When text is linked, the text becomes underlined, indicating a hyperlink (click to go somewhere).

7. Save the pages as you work

    From the time each page is created, save often with *.html* or *.htm* as the file extension.

8. Proof and test the page

    Check the page with an Internet browser to ensure it looks the way you want it to look when it is published. Try all links to be sure they link properly.

9. Publish the page

    Files need to be sent via FTP (File Transfer Protocol) to be stored on the Internet.

10. Test the page on the Internet

    Test in several browsers, and on both Mac and PC. Test the links every few months, as Web sites move or expire frequently.

11. Update pages on a regular basis

Classroom Tip:
If the design of a Web page is a class project, organize students into groups, each with a specific task. Never undertake a Web design project unless you, the teacher, understand all aspects of the project (even though your students might be better at Web page design than you).

11.3 - Creating Classroom Web Pages

Some educational portals provide templates for constructing school Web pages which then can be hosted on the portal's site. Even though your school might have its own school site, it might be fun to have one just for your class(es). You can post homework and announcements and keep in touch with parents. Class Web pages can also include rules and policies, news about the school, teacher/staff e-mail addresses, sports information, upcoming events, fun links for students, school calendars, class schedules, cafeteria menus, sites for homework help, student projects, and much more.

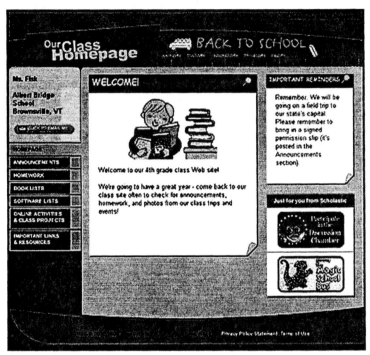

Scholastic's home page, found at (teacher.scholastic.com/homepage builder/index.htm) includes *Class Homepage Builder*. As illustrated here, this looks like a real Web page with columns and boxes for various types of information. Templates are provided to make your page look like this one. You can even include printable parent forms online.

Another site for teachers is *TeAch-nology.com* (www.teach-nology.com/Web_tools/Web_site/). This site provides several categories of Web pages. They do have one for free. With this free subscription, they provide 12 MB of Web space and access to their file manager. This does, however, include advertising (which can be removed for a fee) when displayed on the Web. Their other packages, with fees involved, provide additional space, support FTP or *FrontPage* files and offer Webmail accounts and free support. To see if you want to use it in your classroom, try the free version and use their file manager, which means you use their template to create your Web page (the easy way to do it). They also provide links to sites that offer free cursors, backgrounds, clipart, icons, etc.

4Teachers.org (wizard.4teachers.org) has a *Web Worksheet Wizard* that allows the teacher to create a lesson, worksheet, or class page and publish it on the WWW through *4Teachers.org*. For students, they have *Project Poster* (poster.4teachers.org). This free tool allows students to make online school projects and short reports. They can include one image, four links to other Web pages, and a report of up to 3,500 characters. Students can only post a school project, and they must be registered by their teacher. After being reviewed, the poster is placed on the Web for the public to view.

11.4 - Creating a Web Site with *Netscape Composer*

There are several versions of *Netscape Communicator* available. Any version 7.2 or below includes *Netscape Composer*. This is a free download for both PC and Mac.

1. Open Netscape (if you do not have it, it can be downloaded from www.netscape.com).

2. To access *Composer* and create a new page: go to *File: New: Composer Page*. At the top of the page there is a Composition Toolbar (shown below), along with a Menu Bar. Any time you are editing pages, you must be in *Composer* with this toolbar visible. There is also an Edit Mode Toolbar at the bottom left of the screen.

3. To create a new page within *Composer*: click on *New* in the toolbar.

4. To view your page in a browser to check links: click on *Browse* in the toolbar.

5. To edit your page: go to *File: Edit Page* on the menu bar.

6. To add and change text: type as in a word processor. Sizes and body text styles can be changed in the toolbar. Additional changes can be made under *Format* in the menu bar. Do not use fancy fonts. Times, Arial, Helvetica, and Courier stay the same, while others change on various computers.

7. To save your page: Go to *File: Save*. Enter *index* (Composer will add the *.html*). Save directly to a folder you have created to hold all of your pages and images. All file names must be lowercase; no spaces.

8. To change text and background colors: Text color can be changed in the Format menu in the menu bar. Background and text colors for the entire page can be changed under *Format: Page Colors and Background*. Text and background colors can also be changed in the toolbar. This, however, is not for the entire page; it is only for specific sections. Go to the icon to the right of body text. The left (black) is for text color; the right (white) is for the background color (best not to use).

9. To check spelling: click on *Spell* in the toolbar.

10. To add a table (tables are used for organizing text and images in rows and columns):
    a. click to place the insertion point where the table will appear
    b. click on *Table* in the toolbar
    c. enter the number of rows and columns needed
    d. enter the width of the table (percentage of window)

    e. click *OK*

    f. add or delete rows and columns under *Table: Insert/Delete*

11. To make changes in a table: (first click in table) - go to *Table: Table Properties* in the menu bar (choose *Table* or *Cell*).

    a. in *Table*, change width, alignment, color, border (use 0 pixels for no border)

    b. in *Cells*, change size of cells (use width - % of table to make cells the same width)

12. To add an image: click on *Image* in the toolbar. (Prior to doing this, image files must be in the same folder as your pages. They must have a *.gif* or *.jpeg* (or *.jpeg*) extension.) The menu below will appear. Click on *Choose File*; navigate to your *web page* folder, then open the image. Click on *URL is relative to page location* (if not checked). If you want alternate text to appear if the image does not open, select that option and enter the desired text; if not, click on *Don't use alternate text*.

Image Location:

☐ URL is relative to page location   (**Choose File...**)

Tooltip:

● Alternate text:

○ Don't use alternate text

> *Note:*
>   *Text cannot be placed directly next to pictures, except at the top, bottom, left, right, and center (see illustration).*
>   *To have more flexibility, make a table and put images in the cells.*

text

13. To edit images: double click on the image. You can then change dimensions and appearance (including text location), or make it a link.

14. To give a name to the page (if your page will be on a Web site, label the page with a descriptive title): go to *Format: Page Title and Properties*. This will show at the top of the page and as a bookmark.

15. To create links to Web sites: Highlight the text or image to be the link; click the *Link* button in the toolbar; enter the link location. Be sure to begin the address with *http://*. Be sure *URL is relative to page location* is checked.

16. To create links to other pages: Highlight the text or image to be the link; click the *Link* button in the toolbar; choose the appropriate file; click *Open*, then *OK*.

17. To create links (anchors) in the same page: (anchors link to text in the same page, usually on a long Web page):
    a. Click to set the insertion point at the beginning of the line where you want to create the anchor;
    b. Go to *Insert: Named Anchor*;
    c. Enter a name for your anchor; click *OK*; an anchor appears;
    d. Select the text or image to link to the anchor;
    e. Click *Link* in the toolbar; then click on the *name of the anchor*; click *OK*.

18. To enter your e-mail address: *highlight the text* you want to be the link; click on *Link* in the toolbar; enter: *mailto:youraddress*.

19. To insert previously saved documents: (There are several ways to do this. You need to try each to see the differences. Since you are working in HTML, text cannot easily be copied in while keeping the original formatting.)
    a. Copy and Paste: Copy your original document; paste into the Web page (this will not be formatted correctly).
    b. Save as a Web page: In *Word*, save the document as a Web page (formatting will be better than copy and paste).
    c. Save as a document: Place your *Word* document in your Web page folder. It will not open as a Web page but will be saved as a file on the computer.
    d. Save as a PDF file: In *Word*, go to *Print*, then *Save as PDF*. This will also be saved as a file on the computer.

20. When all is complete, test your site on the Internet, not just through Browse.

Web Publishing

After your Web page is created, it needs to be posted on a Web server. This could be on a school's server, a commercial online service, such as *AOL*, or with an ISP (Internet Service Provider). If you are a subscriber to *AOL, Verizon, Comcast*, or similar providers, they normally provide free space for you to post a Web page. Contact them directly for information. If this service is not available, you can purchase space from a service provider. Some schools will provide free space on their network.

Another alternative is to use a free site on the WWW. Sites for teachers were discussed earlier in the chapter. Other sites also offer free space for Web pages. At these locations, Web sites can be created with their tools or uploaded from another Web authoring program (*Netscape, Dreamweaver*, etc), via an FTP program (provided at their site). Unfortunately, these sites include advertisements when the page is seen. Two of these sites are *Geocities* (geocities.yahoo.com) and *Angelfire* (angelfire.lycos.com).

11.5 - Creating a Web Site with *Microsoft Word*

Microsoft Word is not a full-scale Web authoring program, but it has enough options to construct and publish a simple Web page. *Word* has an option to *Save as Web Page*. When doing this, the page is formatted for the Web. However, the document is not the same. Margins change with the width of the Web document, graphics jump, tabs do not exist, fonts change, spaces disappear, symbols change, and so on. Needless to say, the document does not look the same. A document without graphics, formatting, or special features might transfer in a usable format. When working in *Online Layout* (View), the page is seen as it is viewed on the Web. The feature *Web Page Preview* is also available. Try a document and see what happens! This same concept is true when any word processing document is placed on a Web page.

When choosing to prepare a Web document in *Word*, a better choice is to begin the document as a Web page in the *Project Gallery*. When this is done, many of the same concepts explained for *Netscape Composer* are similar for a Web page in *Word*. Some differences follow:

1. There is a toolbar customized for the Web. Go to *View: Toolbars: Web* to get this toolbar (see below).

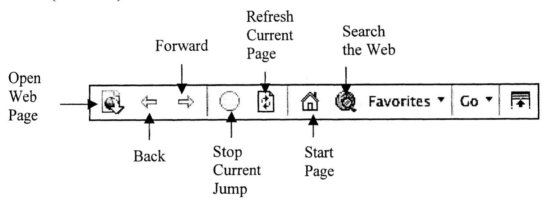

2. When the document is saved, images in the document are converted to *.jpg, .gif,* or *.jpn* files, so they are suitable for the Web; all must be kept together in one folder.

3. To insert a hyperlink, enter and highlight the text. Go to *Insert: Hyperlink* in the menu bar. As illustrated on the next page, enter the entire Web address in *Link to:* Other options shown on the next page are to link to another part of the Web page (*Document*) or to link to an E-mail address.

Insert Hyperlink

Link to: http://www.rowan.edu

Display: Rowan University

Web Page | Document | E-mail Address

4. When saving, ensure the file is saved as a Web page with the *.htm* or *.html* extension.

11.6 - Activities

• Activity One •

Design a Web site for a school. Provide: (1) A home page with basic information and links to other pages. (2) At least six pages that connect from the home page. (3) Information for each page. (4) External links for the students. This is not intended to be a real Web site. This is a planning activity. Draw it out as though you intended to use it in the future. Include a drawing of what would be on each page.

• Activity Two •

Go to *Scholastic's Class Homepage Builder*. Design a home page for a classroom where you are doing (or have done) a field experience.

• Activity Three •

Using *Word* or *Netscape*, design and construct a three-page Web site on any topic. Post it on a free or school server.

Tool
12

Drawing Tools
and
Clip Art

12.1 - Introduction

All digital images–drawings, photos, graphs–are referred to as *graphics*. Graphics software is used to create, edit, or enhance these images. All assist in adding visual images to your projects. Programs to create images fall into two main categories: paint programs, which are used to create bit-mapped images, and drawing programs, which are used to create object-oriented images.

Paint environments are typically for the artist creating artwork and doing illustrations. They employ computer-based paint brushes, air brushes, pencils, and other tools. Using these paint tools, colors and shapes are "painted" on the computer screen as they would be painted onto a canvas. An eraser is available to remove the artwork. Since some artistic ability, along with specialized software, is required for painting, paint will not be covered here.

Drawing tools are commonly used by teachers and students. They are accessible and easy to use. Drawing environments include object-oriented tools such as lines, rectangles, and circles, along with colors, patterns, and textures. Objects can be drawn on the screen, rearranged, and grouped together.

Drawing and painting programs intended for school and personal use (in opposition to high-ended programs for the artist) are a part of the integrated suites *AppleWorks* and *Microsoft Works*. In these packages, the drawing tools can also be found as components of word processing. The drawing tools illustrated in this unit are components of *Word* and *PowerPoint* in *Microsoft Office* (*Office* does not include painting). Tools in all programs are similar. Once you understand the basics, you can use the tools in any program.

Students can use drawing tools to add interest to writing samples, newsletters, and report covers; draw maps; and develop concept maps, graphs and tables, and organizational charts. Teachers can create classroom plans and seating charts and design bulletin boards, learning centers, flyers, and signs, to mention a few uses.

Clip art includes all ready-made graphics that can be added to documents, signs, flyers, newsletters, cards, Web pages, etc. for interest and creativity. Some clip art is available free of charge, while other clip art is available commercially. Given the large number of choices, it is

often time consuming to locate just the right graphic. Some sources of free clip art are included in this chapter. Teachers and students can make use of clip art to enhance any document, such as newsletters, bulletins, reports, projects, worksheets, instructional handouts, and displays.

Graphic editing software is used to edit and enhance graphic objects. *Photoshop®* is often used for this. An easier version of the program, *Photoshop Elements*, is also available. While these programs are complex and often time-consuming to learn, they are not always necessary. *Word* has a variety of image-editing tools powerful enough for correcting and editing digital photographs, scanned images, and clip art.

12.2 - Using the Drawing Tools

The Drawing Toolbar in *Word* and *PowerPoint* is normally found at the left of the screen. If the toolbar is not visible, go to *View: Toolbars: Drawing* on the Menu Bar.

Drawing Toolbars

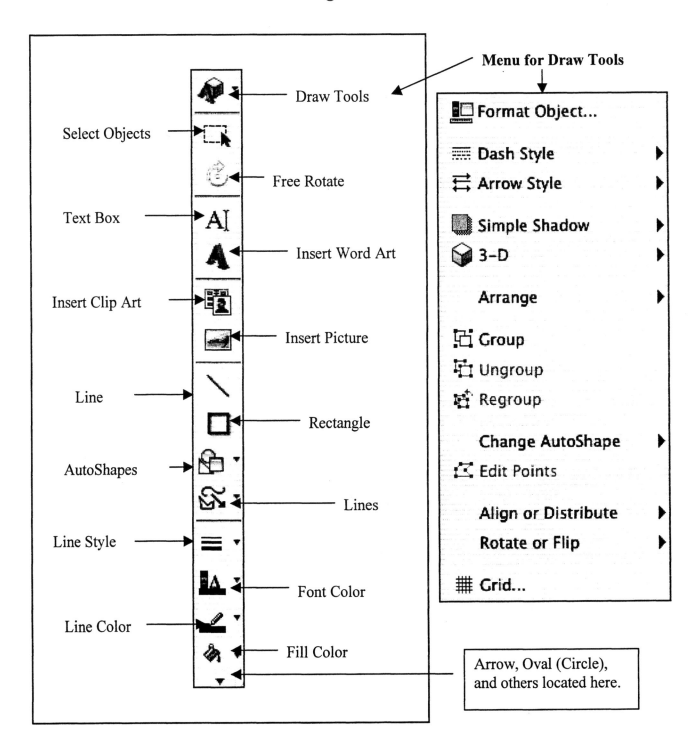

The Drawing Tools

Drawing an Object: Choose the line, rectangle, or oval tool. Place the cursor on the screen where the object is to begin. Holding down the mouse button, drag to form the object; release the mouse button when the size is complete. To draw a straight line, a square, or a circle, hold down the Shift key while dragging. To draw more than one of the same object, double click the tool prior to drawing.

Modifying Objects: To move or change objects once they are drawn, click on the Select Objects Tool (Pointer), then click on the object.

Handles will appear on the object, making it active.

With the object active:
- to resize the object, drag a handle;
- to move the object, click inside (with the hand) and drag;
- to delete the object, use the delete key.

Line Width and Style: Thickness (and styles) of the line (or outline) drawn can be changed with the Line Style Tool. Make the item active; choose the width or style desired. Lines can be changed to multiple lines with the style tool or dashes with the dash tool.

Object and Line Colors: Color palettes, along with fill effects such as gradients, textures, and patterns, are available to fill and color objects and lines.
 Fill Color places color (and other fills) inside the object.
 Line Color places color or patterns on the line or outline of the object.

Font Colors: Apply colors to highlighted text in word processing or active text in a text box.

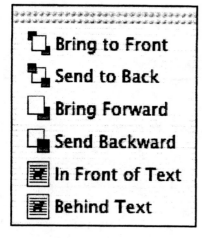

Rotate/Flip: Once clip art, or another graphical object, is inserted, the art can be rotated using the Free Rotate Tool, or rotated/flipped through this menu in the Draw Tools. First select the object, then choose the rotation or flip to be used.

114

Word Art: Text is formatted in a variety of preset styles to add interest to any document or presentation.

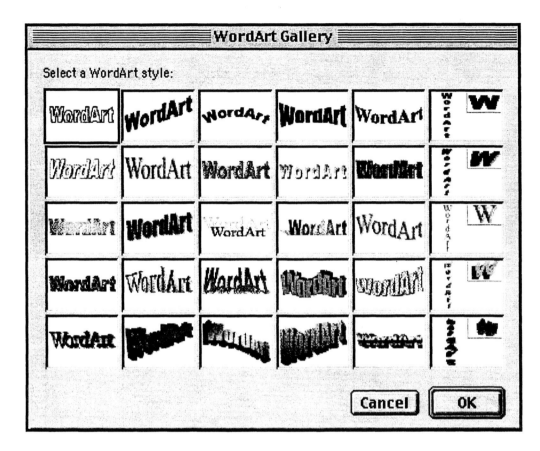

When a style is chosen and text is added, the Word Art is shown, along with the Word Art Toolbar. Colors can be selected, sizing modified, shapes changed and rotated, and more.

Insert Clip Art and Picture: Clip art from *Word* in inserted through *Clip Art*, while clip art files, photos, scanned objects, or any other external objects can be inserted through *Picture*. Images can be inserted from the Drawing Toolbar or Formatting Palette, or from *Insert: Picture* on the Menu Bar. The top graphic here indicates *Clip Art*; the bottom, *Picture*.

Shadows and 3-D: Once an object is drawn, shadows or three-dimensional effects can be added. Select the object; choose the Shadow or 3-D Tool from the Draw Tools.

Text Boxes: Text entered in a text box becomes a graphic and can be manipulated like other graphics. It can be moved to various locations or grouped with objects for identification. When the box is active (handles), text can be changed in the same way as when text is highlighted in word processing. The direction of the text can also be changed.

AutoShapes: Graphical shapes that can be added in the same way rectangles and ovals are drawn. In the *AutoShape* menu, there are five categories of shapes (below). Choose the shape to use, then drag the mouse to draw the shape.

Basic Shapes are shown on the right, with one example below.

Arrows: With handles on a line or arrow, select *Arrow Style* to make arrows in various styles and directions. The Line Style Tool can be used to change the thickness of the line.

Arranging Objects: Objects appear on the screen in the order they are drawn. To change this order and create various effects, the objects can be arranged. Click on the object; choose *Arrange* in the Draw Tools; move as appropriate.

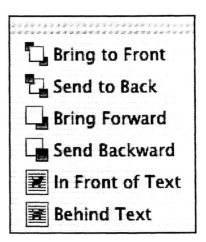

Aligning Objects: To have objects line up on the left or right, the bottom or top, or distribute space between them, use *Align* or *Distribute* in the Draw Tools.

Grouping Objects: When several objects are going to be used together (including text made in a text box), they can be grouped together. When grouped, they all move together for ease of formatting the screen.

To group objects, click on each object to be included while holding down the Shift key; handles will appear on all objects. An alternative is to drag the Select Object Tool around all objects (like putting a rectangle around all objects). Choose *Group* in the Draw Tools. When grouped, there will be handles around the group, not each object. To take apart, choose *Ungroup* in the Draw Tools.

Design and Draw a Classroom (using tools in any drawing program)

As a part of your education program, an assignment might be to draw and/or design a classroom. This can be done with the drawing tools explained above. Seating charts can also be developed and easily modified. The drawing tools can be used to draw room furniture, doors, windows, and other components. When more than one of an item is needed, copy or duplicate the item rather than trying to replicate it with the drawing tools. For instance: draw a desk; copy and paste it to make more. Make a row of desks; group them; then copy for additional rows.

Make use of textures and fills to indicate specific items. Use the text tool for labeling. A symbol key can be added for easy identification.

Additional icons for furniture, office supplies, computers, etc., can be found on clip art CDs/DVDs or at clip art sites on the Internet.

12.3 - Using Graphics (Clip Art)

 Graphics software (often termed "clip art") includes packaged collections of graphics, usually indexed into libraries by topic. This term originated when art was "clipped" and pasted into documents. Most software (such as *Microsoft Office* and *AppleWorks*) that uses graphics elements contains clip art libraries. In addition to that in the software programs, CDs or DVDs with thousands of images can be purchased. Much more can be located on the Internet. Clip art can be used by the teacher to enhance any document. While there are probably millions of pieces of clip art available, it is often difficult to locate just what you want.

File Formats

Print clip art falls into one of two graphical image categories: bitmapped or vector. Bitmapped images, also known as raster, can only be edited in paint or bitmap editing programs. This limits their resolutions to the size in which they were created. Enlarging the graphic makes it look worse; lines appear jagged. Reducing size does not improve the image; it stays the same. Typical file formats for these are *.bmp* (bitmapped), *.pict* (picture format), and *.tiff* (Tagged Image File). Vector images, also referred to as object-oriented images, are more versatile. These graphics can be edited in draw or object-oriented editing programs. These appear the same at any resolution; their appearance does not change with resizing. Typical file formats for these are *.esp* (encapsulated postscript) and *.pict* (which can also be bitmapped).

Graphics for the Internet are typically *.gif* (Graphics Interchange Format) or *.jpeg* (Joint Photographic Experts Group) formats. *.gif* requires less storage space than bitmapped images. It only allows for 256 colors and is used for simple images. *.jpeg* is usually used for photos on the Web and allows for millions of colors.

These file formats will appear after the name of the clip art as an extension. If clip art is not in the correct format for use in a program, it can be translated using a graphic conversion program. Many of these can be found on the Internet as shareware or freeware programs.

Sources of Clip Art

Clip art, available as black and white images, photography, color line art, maps, borders, icons, or cartoons, can be acquired from a variety of sources.

Many application programs, such as *Microsoft Office, AppleWorks, HyperStudio®, The Print Shop®, Kid Pix®,* etc. include their own clip art libraries. To utilize clip art in *Microsoft Office*, go to the Insert Menu; choose *Picture: Clip Art*. A library of clip art will appear. Choose the category of interest. When a piece of clip art is selected, click on it, then choose *Insert*. At this same location, choosing *Online* will take you to Microsoft's online *Clip Art and Media* site, featuring clip art in various categories.

Other clip art can be purchased on CDs/DVDs. When accessing clip art from CDs, DVDs, and other programs, click on the object; *Edit: Copy* (puts the graphic into the memory of the computer); go to the document where you want the clip art: *Edit: Paste*. The clip art is transferred to this document. *Word* also has the option of using *Insert: Picture: From File*. After choosing this, locate the clip art on a CD, in a file, on a disk, etc. Photos and scanned images are also inserted in this way.

There is a multitude of free clip art available on the WWW. There are sites where clip art can be downloaded at no cost, while other sites are by subscription only. Many of the free sites are full of advertisements, making it difficult to locate the clip art. The sites below are for teachers and students, with easy to find and use clip art. Additional links are on the *Technology Tools for Teachers* Web site.

Awesome Clipart for Educators	www.awesomeclipartforeducators.com/
Classroom Clipart	classroomclipart.com/
Discovery School	school.discovery.com/clipart/index.html
Kaboose™	www.kidsdomain.com/clip/
School Clip Art	www.school-clip-art.com/
Teacher Files	www.teacherfiles.com/clip_art.htm

Another source for free clip art is from *Images* files located on Web browsers such as *Google* (www.google.com), *Yahoo* (search.yahoo.com/images), and *AltaVista* (www.altavista.com). The screen for *Google* is below. Click on *Images*; enter the topic to search for; *Search Images*. Limit your topic as much as possible or you could end up with millions of images. (a search for "book" found over five million images).

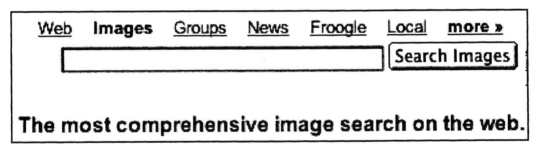

AltaVista Image Search provides even more choices.

Downloading Web Clip Art

Clip art from the Web can be placed in documents in two ways: (1) inserted directly into the document and (2) saved to disk (or computer), then inserted. When working with a document in *Word*, or other word processors, any of these methods can be used. If inserting to a Web-based document, the image must be downloaded to disk, with the original file staying in the same folder as the Web page.

- Locate the clip art on the WWW
- Hold down the mouse button (PC = right button) for several seconds, or hold down the Control key while clicking on the clip art
- The menu to the right will appear with options to copy, download, etc.
- If the document where you want to place the clip art is open, choose *Copy Image* on the Web menu, then return to the document where the clip art is to go
- *Edit: Paste* into the document
- Most programs also support *Drag and Drop*, where you can drag the image to the file where it will be used
- The clip art can also be saved to the hard drive of the computer or on a disk to use at a later time

> **Open Link in New Window**
> **Download Link to Disk**
> **Copy Link to Clipboard**
> **Add Link to Favorites**
>
> **Open Image in New Window**
> **Download Image to Disk**
> **Copy Image**
> **Reload Image**

Adding Clip Art to a Document

When any type of clip art, photo, or scanned image is placed in a word processing document, it is "in line" with the text. The size can be changed, but it cannot be moved or edited. The graphic must be changed to a "floating" graphic. To do this:

- Double click on the image (or go to *Format: Picture*)
- In the Format Picture menu, click on *Layout*
- Choose any of the selections except "Inline with text"
- Click on *OK*
- Position the graphic within the text (text wrap will also now take place)

Resizing and Moving Images

Once an image is "floating," it has "handles." To resize an object proportionately, drag any corner handle. To resize an object proportionately, drag any middle handle. Move the object by "grabbing" with the Hand Tool at the edge or center of the object.

12.4 - Editing Images

Using the image editing tools in *Word*, it is possible to edit images (photos, scanned images, and bitmapped pictures images) usually edited in *Photoshop* or other editing programs. Editing tools can be accessed from the Picture Toolbar (*View: Toolbars*), *Edit: Edit Picture*, or the Formatting Palette.

Row 1:
> *Format Picture*: sets image size, text wrap, brightness, contrast, and more.
> *Free Rotate*: (also available in the Drawing Toolbar); Click on a green handle and rotate in any direction.

Row 2:
> *Effects:* applies a special effects filter to the image (or part of it).
> *Simple Shadow:* adds a shadow behind the image.

Row 3:
> *Image Control:* converts the image to grayscale or black-and-white. *Watermark* dims the picture and places it in the background.
> *Contrast* and *Brightness* icons reduce or intensify contrast or brightness.

Row 4:
> *Set Transparent Color:* makes a specific color transparent.
> *Color Adjustment*: adjusts colors or their saturation.
> *Fix Red Eye:* eliminates red eye in photos.
> *Remove Scratch:* eliminates a scratch in a photo or scan.
> *Crop:* removes unnecessary material from around an object (cannot change size later).

Row 5: [Tools to select a portion of an object for editing.]
> *Cutout*: cuts out the unused area selected by the tools below.
> *Rectangular* and *Oval Marquee:* select an area to use.
> *Lassos:* select irregular-shaped areas to use.

(see examples on the next page)

| Oval Marquee | Rectangular Marquee | Lasso |

12.5 - Activities

• Activity One •

Using the drawing tools and clip art, replicate a classroom where you are doing your field experience. Include seating, equipment, computers, windows, doors, teacher area, storage, bookcases, etc. Clip art from the Web can be used for any of the items.

• Activity Two •

Visit five good Web sites for clip art: (1) Review what is available at each site for a teacher to use in the classroom. (2) Copy an image from each into a *Word* document. (3) Using a text box, identify the site where each was found.

• Activity Three •

Produce a worksheet for a lesson you are teaching. Include at least two drawing tools, two pieces of clip art, and two text boxes.

• Activity Four •

Take several photos with a digital camera. Choose the two best photos. For one, use the Crop Tool to crop out the best part of the picture. For the other, crop it using the Oval and Rectangular Marquees and the Lasso, as in the pictures above. Place them on one page and print out.

Tool

13

Digital Images and Video

13.1 - Introduction

Having a computer in the classroom is only the beginning of what you and your students can do with technology. Digital input and output devices expand the possibilities for using digital images in projects and presentations. Photos can be taken, edited, and printed using a digital camera and peripherals; photos and documents can be scanned for manipulation with the computer; and text can be input without using the keyboard. Any of these images, or anything on the computer, can be sent to a large screen via a video (LCD) projector. These images are stored on CDs, DVDs, or USB minidrives.

Digital video and audio also play an important role in the field of multimedia, as quality video and audio files can be input as files on the computer. Once in the computer, these files can be edited and manipulated to be used in various ways. Titles, music, narration, and transitions can be added. After editing, they can be made into movies.

To use video in the computer, the images must first be captured with a video camera, then digitized to use in the computer. The first technology for this was video sent to the computer from a VCR, or other video device, through a video capture card in the computer. Today, video from a VCR can be digitized for use in the computer. The latest technology is the digital video (DV) camcorder, which eliminates digitizing or the need for a video capture card in the computer. Video from the DV camcorder is sent to the computer via a special cable, known as a FireWire® cable (the computer must have a FireWire port).

Once in the computer, the video is edited using video-editing software. Clips can be arranged in any order; visual effects can be added; and audio in the form of musical soundtracks, voiceovers, or sound effects can be included. Programs such as *iMovie* for Macintosh (free as a part of *iLife* on new Macs) and *Movie Maker* (free as a part of *Windows XP*) for PCs make this a simple process. Edited movies can be stored back on the DV tape; put on a videotape, CD or DVD; shared with friends and relatives via e-mail; used on Web pages; or used as components of presentations. Placing the finished product on a disk for a presentation is not an option. Digital video requires an enormous amount of storage space. A five-minute clip takes over one gigabyte of storage space on the computer.

The video camera and video editing are covered in separate sections after digital input and output devices.

13.2 - Digital Input

Any device that allows the user to enter data, commands, and responses to the computer is termed an input device. Common to every computer is the keyboard and the mouse (laptops, however, have a built-in keyboard and a trackpad in place of a mouse). Other input devices include digital cameras, scanners, electronic whiteboards, touch screens, digital tablets and pens, and more. Once in the computer, the images can be modified with photo editing programs, or in paint or drawing environments. The finished products can be used in various ways.

Digital Cameras

As input devices, digital cameras take pictures that can immediately be saved on a memory card or in the camera, imported into the computer or saved on a disk or a CD for use as a graphic in any application program at a later time, and printed on a home printer or at a processing location for immediate prints. Cameras and/or memory cards can hold hundreds of photos, depending on their size. Less expensive than traditional photos, digital cameras do not require film, thus eliminating processing charges. They are easy to use, even by children. Unwanted photos can be deleted, and photos can be retaken immediately.

 When photos are taken, they are usually stored on a memory card within the camera. This card can then be placed in a slot in the computer, or in a card reader that goes into a USB port in the computer, for easy access. Cameras without the memory card are linked to the computer via a USB cable to import the photos into the computer. This method limits the number of photos that can be taken. Using memory cards, the larger the storage capacity of the card, the more photos that can be stored. You can also use several cards before downloading the photos to the computer. Software within the computer transfers the images to the hard drive of the computer, or they can be directly accessed from the memory card.

Most digital cameras store pictures as *.jpeg* files, so pictures can easily be sent to friends and family via e-mail, manipulated with editing software, or placed on a Web page. If a digital camera is not available, pictures taken with a 35mm camera can also be processed for use in a computer. When film is processed, photos can be stored on a CD-ROM (PhotoCD) and can be accessed in the same way as those taken with a digital camera.

Camera Features

One of the first things to look for in a camera is the image resolution. Image quality is measured in pixels; in cameras, it is measured in Mega Pixels (MP=million pixels), with the image quality increasing as the number increases. Cameras suitable for classroom and personal use are basic point-and-shoot models, with the MP being under six. Other "high-end varieties" are available for professionals. The point-and-shoot cameras do not have as many features as the more expensive models, but most tend to take quality photos. These cameras are adequate for Web pages and snapshots. A resolution of 640 x 480 pixel images is high enough for pictures used for e-mail and web pages.

Prices are dependent on features included (red eye reduction, auto-focus, flash, self-timer, zoom), image resolution, method of storing photos, number of images that can be stored (in camera, on card, or on disk), type of lenses, LCD screen for viewing (see large image on screen, as well as in viewfinder), and capability of storing video clips as well as photos.

Using a Digital Camera (instructions for the *Canon A520*; similar for other cameras)

1. Insert batteries.
2. Insert the memory card (if applicable).
3. Press the Power Button to turn the camera on.
4. Slide the Mode Switch to the *camera* icon.
5. Turn the Shooting Mode Dial to AUTO.
6. Aim the camera at the subject.
7. Adjust the Zoom Lever.
8. Press the Shutter Button half way to focus (beeps twice).
9. Press the Shutter Button all the way to shoot the picture.
10. To playback the pictures: Slide the Mode Switch to the *arrow*; use the Select Buttons to display the images.
11. To erase a picture: Press the Function Button (right of the Menu Button); check that *Erase* is selected; press the SET Button (between Select Buttons).
12. Check the instruction book for more detailed instructions.

Downloading Pictures to the Computer

1. Install the software that comes with the camera (Macintosh–photos can be downloaded directly into *iPhoto*®).
2. Connect the camera to the computer using the USB cable that comes with the camera.
3. Slide the Mode Switch to Playback *(arrow);* turn the camera on.
4. The software should recognize the camera and appear (if not, locate the software from the *Start Menu* on a PC, or *Applications* on a Mac).
5. Download the images, following the directions on the menus.

Using a Memory Card

1. Eject the memory card from the camera.
2. Insert it into a slot in the computer, or into a memory card reader that goes into the USB port of the computer.
3. Double click the icon of the drive, or memory card, containing the pictures.
4. Copy the images to a folder for use at a later time.

Image Editing Software

Once a digital picture or image is imported into the computer, it can be edited in various programs. Image editing software can be used, along with easy-to-use drawing and painting programs. New versions of *Microsoft Word* include editing tools (see Tool 12: Drawing Tools and Clip Art). *Adobe PhotoShop* is the standard for high-end image editing. While this program is quite complex, Adobe's *PhotoShop Elements* is easier for students and teachers to use. These programs provide selection tools, touch-up features, special effects, tools to crop and resize, and ways to brighten or lighten the photo or image. Some programs also provide templates and backgrounds for fun themes and special occasions.

***iPhoto* for Macintosh OSX**

Part of *iLife*® for Macintosh is *iPhoto*. Images can be imported from a digital camera, PhotoCD, or any other source. By plugging a digital camera into a Macintosh with *iPhoto*, photos are automatically loaded into the software. Icons on the Menu Bar below assist in editing, organizing, printing, and sharing photos.

When importing photos, you are given the option to erase the photos after they are imported. However, you should wait to be sure they are successfully downloaded before doing this, They can then be erased from the camera. When importing, a name can be given to the group of photos as they are imported (e.g. Student Portfolios, May, 2006). Movie clips can also be imported. Once imported, you can view the photos, delete those you do not want to keep, organize them into folders, or create an instant slide show.

Scanners

Scanners are light-sensing devices, attached to a computer in a USB port, that read documents, photos, and more. Similar in concept to copy machines, they copy a page at a time, producing a graphic image. Images are then sent to the computer and saved in a file format such as .*tiff*, .*jpeg*, .*gif*, .*pict*, according to their end use. Print images are, therefore, translated to digital images.

Text can also be scanned; however, the end product is still a graphic image. The image can be digitized by OCR (Optical Character Recognition) software for editing in a word processing program. This conversion does not always produce satisfactory results. Accuracy is limited to the fonts used in the original text and the type of document formatting. When the digitized text is opened in a word processor it is often thrown around on the page, and some text is not even recognizable. Higher quality OCR software often produces more accurate results.

Most scanners today are flatbed scanners. There is a glass plate under the lid with a light under it. Light passes under the bed, producing a computer image. Each scanned image is made up of many dots, with resolution measured in dots per inch (DPI). It does not matter if the scanned image is a photograph, magazine, line art, text, or a map; it is made of dots, not lines or letters.

When a scanner is purchased, it comes with software that needs to be installed on the computer. If it is not available, most of it can be downloaded from the manufacturer's site on the Internet.

Images are saved and edited in much the same way as those from digital cameras. Saving as .*tiff* produces a very large document and is not recommended when disk space is an issue. Anything used for the Internet or e-mail must be saved as .*gif* or .*jpeg*. All photos must be saved as .*jpeg*.

Graphics Tablets, Pens, and Touch Screens

A graphics tablet or pad can be attached to the computer. Graphics tablets allow students to create artwork on the tablet, then import the work into the computer. Text can also be recognized by the computer and imported into a word processing document.

Pens, such as those in PDAs, take handwritten notes and place them into a word processor document. The same concept is used in tablet PCs. Although they are a little larger, choices are made and work is done with a stylus.

A touch screen allows the user to input text by touching the screen with a finger or pointer. Often used by the physically impaired who cannot use keyboards, touching icons, on a touch-sensitive screen, provides input to the computer.

Electronic Whiteboards

Electronic whiteboards are often found in classrooms. With the standard models, you can digitally capture anything created on the whiteboard. This can then be transferred to the computer and saved or printed. In the classroom, these are often used for discussions and brainstorming sessions, with the products saved and printed for the students.

Becoming more commonplace in classrooms today is the interactive electronic whiteboard. Often called "smart boards" (SMART™ Technologies, Inc. first introduced these boards in 1991), this technology allows a computer image to be projected onto the board. Touching the board (instead of using a mouse) operates the software and manipulates the software.

Using the interactive whiteboard, you can run and display computer programs, surf the Web, and "use" the computer on the whiteboard as you would on the computer itself. Sounds can be heard, and video images can be displayed. Anything on the board can be written over. Software that comes with the boards make it possible to move and manipulate text and objects on the board, save information, and convert handwriting to text. With the built-in scanner, everything on the screen can digitally captured and sent back to the computer to be saved, printed, etc.

Along with a computer and the whiteboard, a digital projector is also needed for projection. Information from the computer is displayed by the projector onto the touch-sensitive whiteboard instead of the computer monitor.

Using an interactive whiteboard, the teacher can be in front of the class (and the board), rather than behind the computer. Students are a big part of the lesson, as they come to the board to enter their own answers and comments. By participating, they feel more a part of their education. They can touch the whiteboard with their finger or a stylus and write notes and comments whenever needed. Since everything on the interactive whiteboard can be saved to the computer and printed, students can pay more attention to what is going on in class and get notes printed out later. Students with special needs are also at an advantage, as they can touch the screen instead of attempting to work with a keyboard. Computer images are also much easier for them to view.

More information can be obtained about SMART Boards at www.smarttech.com. Here you can find out about different types of boards and access educational materials. Their Educator Resources features Lesson Activities (hundreds of interactive lesson activities, along with correlated standards), Software Resources, Community (share with other educators using SMART products), Professional Development, and Online Classroom Resources (Web sites with free, curriculum-related resources for the classroom)

Hand-held Computing Devices

Personal Digital Assistants (PDAs), Palms, Pocket/Personal PCs, Hand-held Computers, and Hand-held Devices all fall into the category of Hand-held Computing Devices. Small like a cellular phone or pocket gaming device, these are new tools found in today's classrooms. They might contain a personal organizer, a word processor, a digital camera, Internet and e-mail connectivity, and several types of calculators all in one device for the price of a graphing calculator. In addition to these capabilities, free and inexpensive software can be obtained for use in the K-12 classroom. Probes are available for science classes, concept mapping is available for language arts, databases of historical facts can be downloaded for research, and eBooks can be downloaded for reading.

 Built-in features include an on-screen keyboard (a larger, external, keyboard can be added), character recognition (data written with a stylus is interpreted and recognized), synchronization (to communicate with a computer), and an infrared port (to transfer programs and data between units). Text is entered using a stylus and a stylized print format called *Graffiti*. Users learn to input stylized letters that can be recognized and transferred to a word processor. Data is synchronized with a computer via a charge/cradle or a USB cable. Output can also be "beamed" to a printer using infrared signals.

Advantages are low cost, size, ease of use, and mobility. Concerns expressed by school administrators include cheating (beam information to others), compatibility, distraction (students do not pay attention to other things), screen size, and security.

Webcams

Mounted on top of the computer, or built-in to newer models of computers, webcams make video chats easy and inexpensive. As illustrated on the right, some cameras sit on top of the computer. Apple's *iSight*® camera, used in the same way, is illustrated below. New Macintosh computers have an *iSight* camera built in above the display. Less than a half inch in diameter, this functions the same as external cameras. With one of these cameras and appropriate software (*iChat*® for Macintosh), you can videoconference with anyone anywhere in the world. Previously used only for communication (no storage), *iSight* conferences can now be recorded as movies and imported into *iMovie*®. In opposition to older technologies, communication can be full screen, with up to four individuals conferencing.

 Students can collaborate with students around the world, or the teacher can bring "experts" into the classroom. Students can ask questions, share concerns, or show their work to others without going on a field trip or bringing a speaker into the classroom. Teachers can also use video conferencing to apply for jobs, observe other teachers in their classrooms, or share their teaching practices with pre-service teachers.

13.3 - Digital Output: Video Projectors

After data has been input into the computer, it is processed to become output. This can be seen on a monitor, printed on a printer, or listened to through speakers or headsets. Output to be viewed by a large audience can be transmitted through a video projector and shown on a large screen. These can be mounted in the classroom, or serve a portable units to move from one room to another.

Research has shown that large screen projection is more appealing to students than viewing images on either a monitor or a small screen. The video projector makes large screen projection an option for the teacher. Used in classrooms, lecture halls, and auditoriums, this technology works best in a darkened room unless the projector has high lumens. In addition to their use with computers, video projectors can be used with VCRs, visual presenters, DVDs, and any other technology that has a video output jack.

Video projectors can be portable or they can be mounted in the classroom. Because of their small size, they can easily be transported within the school or taken out of the school for presentations at other locations. Most video projectors weigh beween five to ten pounds; however, newer portable models weigh between three to five pounds. The newest video projectors use Digital Light Processing (DLP), a space-saving alternative.

How to Use Video Projectors

Video projectors are available in many models. The instruction manual for the specific model being used should be consulted for the correct connection/use directions. These directions will usually consist of two series of steps: (1) how and where to connect the various cables and (2) How to focus, use, and control the projection display or image. Generally, the technology being coupled with the projector is hooked directly to the projector with a video cable. Computer users will need a special cable that comes with the projector to convert the computer image to a form the projector can display.

Selection Considerations

Brightness:
The brightness of a video projector is measured in ANSI lumens, with higher lumens being more desirable. Lumens under 1,000 usually require the room's lights being off or dimmed. Projectors with brighter lumens are more expensive but provide brighter projection and eliminate the need to dim the lights.

Image Quality:
The resolution of the projector should be compatible with that of the computer being used. Most of these have XGA resolutions. It is important to check the uniformity of brightness and contrast between black and white.

Size and Weight:
The lighter the projector, the easier it is to carry. Select a projector with a sturdy carrying case. If it will be mounted, the projector size must be compatible with a mounting bracket.

Use with a Laptop

When the projector is connected to a laptop, an occurring problem is getting the computer image on the computer screen and the projection screen simultaneously. Users often have to choose specific keyboard commands to export a signal to the projector. It may mean choosing a Simulscan command or using the function key with another key that represents the monitor. Usually a function key between five and eight is the one needed for simulscan. Consult the user's manual. Because of this problem, it is best to first connect and turn on the projector, then turn on the computer.

13.4 - Digital Storage

Storage devices permit the user to store and access documents and programs. While many of these disk drives are internal, or built-in, external disk drives and other storage devices can be added to the computer system. The hard disk drive is where all programs and data are stored, completely enclosed in the computer itself. Currently sized in terms of gigabytes (GB), the larger the drive, the greater the amount of information that can be stored. To input programs and files, CD drives are the standard internal drive for computers today. Most of these can read and/or write DVDs.

Storage Devices

If you are working between computers, data from the hard drive must be made portable, using the one of the following storage devices. The 5.25" floppy disk drive was the original external storage device, followed by 3.5" drives, Zip and Jazz drives, CDs, and DVDs. Newer storage devices are USB (Universal Serial Bus) minidrives, also known as flash drives, keychain drives, jump drives, etc., and memory cards.

 Floppy disks, 3.5" in diameter, contain a magnetic media that has read/write capabilities (read from it, or write to it). A high density disk holds 1.44 MB of data, or approximately 720 pages of text.

Media Equivalencies

3.5 " Floppy Disk =
720 pages of text =
1.4 MB memory

100 MB Zip Disk =
70 Floppy Disks =
50,000 pages of text

CD =
250,000 pages of text =
400 3.5" disks =
6-100 MB Zip disks =
650 MB memory

DVD=
2-8 hours
high quality video=
4.7 GB - 17 GB memory

Zip disks are thicker than floppy disks, holding from 100 MB to 750 MB of data. The 100 MB disk is equivalent to 70 floppy disks.

Compact Disks (CDs) are built-in to most computers. It is necessary to have a CD drive in the computer to install most programs onto the computer. CD-ROM is Read Only Memory; these cannot be written to. CD-R are recordable, and CD-RW are rewritable. The main way to save files as backups or storage (such as photos) is now to "burn" a CD. One CD can hold 650 MB of data, or 250,000 pages of text. CD-RW are the most economical to use, as you can reuse them; CD-R can only be written on once.

Digital Versatile Discs (DVDs) are the newest high capacity CD-size discs used for storage of movies, games, audio, and multimedia. DVD drives are becoming common in computers, with the same drive also playing CDs. Similar to CDs, there is also a recordable format available for storage of large amounts of data, such a classroom-produced movies, music, etc. DVD-Video does not lose audio or video quality with extended use, as do VHS tapes. Storage is from 4.7 GB to 17 GB; 2-8 hours of high-quality video.

USB Minidrives (Flash Drives, Jump Drives, etc.) and Memory Cards are small portable storage units. Flash drives are available in 256 MB - 2 GB (and higher) sizes, while memory cards, used primarily to store digital photos, begin at 16 MB. The higher the number of MB, the more photos that can be stored. The resolution of the camera must also be considered. The higher the resolution, the more memory the pictures take up. A camera with a resolution of 3.2, taking high quality photos, produces 1.5 MB files, while a camera with a resolution of 6.3 produces files of over 3 MB. Therefore, a 16 MB card cannot hold many photos.

Using CDs and DVDs

CD and DVD players are easy to use. The disc is placed on a platform in the computer or DVD player with the shiny side down. An icon identifying the CD or DVD appears on (a) the desktop of the computer (Mac), or (b) in "My Computer" on the desktop of a PC. It can then be opened and ejected in the same manner as a disk. When the disc is opened, most will display a menu of choices for the user. Click and go: it's that easy!

13.5 - Digital Video Camcorders

Digital video (DV) camcorders are the result of a merger of digital cameras and video cameras. They allow the consumer to make their own movies to use on their computer, put on Web pages to share with others, or merely edit and save for school or family use. DV camcorders also take still images. Video and still images are saved as DV formats, making pictures sharper than those taken with VHS camcorders.

DV camcorders are not totally digital; they store the signal in a digital form, while still recording on videotape. The tape used, the "mini-DV," is the smallest videotape. The camcorder is also smaller than any of the other types, but the quality is higher than other video formats. With more features than analog cameras, they provide better zoom, sound, and more control over color and lighting. Tapes can be copied many times without losing quality; they can also be re-recorded many times. The final product takes up 15-30 GB of hard drive space per hour of tape; however, the editing process could take 100 GB (input, saving, editing, output). Many DV camcorders also take memory cards, where still images are stored.

Using a Digital Video Camcorder

(Instructions are for the Canon *Elura 80*; they are similar for other DV camcorders. See the instruction manual with your DV camcorder for more detailed instructions.)
>   **Use tapes labeled *miniDV*.**

Attaching and Charging the Battery Pack

1. Raise the front viewfinder. Insert the battery into the camcorder under the front viewfinder (press lightly and slide it in the direction of the arrow until it clicks).
2. Connect the power cord to the adapter; plug the power cord into a power outlet.
3. Connect the power adapter to the camcorder's DC IN terminal (the *Charge Indicator* starts flashing; it glows steadily when charging is complete).
4. When charging is complete, remove the battery by pressing the *Battery Release* button.
5. To save the battery, the camcorder can be used while plugged in.
6. It takes approximately two hours for the battery to charge. This provides approximately one hour of recording time.

To Record and Review a Movie

1. Open the cassette compartment by sliding the *Open/Eject* switch on the top of the camera.
2. Load the cassette with the window facing the handle. (Pull straight out to eject.)
3. Press the *Push* mark unit it clicks and the tape retracts.
4. Turn the camcorder on; remove the lens cap.
5. To begin recording a movie, set the camcorder to the *Camera* mode.
6. Open the LCD Viewfinder screen by pushing the *Open* button.

Canon Elura 80
(other brands/models are similar)

Viewfinder Side

Battery

LCD
Viewfinder
screen

Record,
Search, and
other buttons
(under
Viewfinder)

Set dial

Menu
button

Zoom lever

Print/share
button

Photo button

Tape/Card
switch

Controls on
top; Viewfinder

DC IN
terminal

P Easy

Program
selector

Power
switch

POWER
NETWORK
PLAY (VCR)
OFF
CAMERA

Power switch
choices

Start/Stop
button

Controls on handle side

135

7. Set the Tape/Card switch to *Tape* (picture of a tape). (*Card* records photos on the memory card; *Tape* records on the DV tape.)
8. Press the *Start/Stop* button to record (and stop recording).
9. When finished, turn the power off. Close the LCD panel, replace the lens cap, and remove the cassette and battery.

To Play Back a Tape

1. Set the camcorder to *Play* (VCR mode). Be sure the *Tape/Card* switch is set to *Tape*.
2. Open the LCD panel.
3. Press and hold the *Record/Search* buttons (top row, left, under the LCD panel). These will rewind (first button) and fast forward (second button) through the tape for viewing.
4. Press the third button to begin playing the tape.
5. Press the fourth button to stop playback.

To Record Still Images (on a Memory Card)

1. Insert the memory card.
2. Set the camcorder to the *Card* mode.
3. Press the *Photo* button halfway. A beep sounds twice indicating focus has occurred.
4. Press the *Photo* button fully.
5. Remove the card and follow instructions in Chapter 14 for working with the images.

13.6 - Digital Video Editing

Digital video editing is the process by which video from a camcorder is taken apart and put back together in another sequence or format. Instead of using all of the video shot, the best parts of it are used and embellished to produce a small movie to be used for a multimedia presentation, shared on the Internet, or saved for other uses.

Video editing software is used to edit the video and audio clips downloaded from a digital camcorder to the computer (or video digitized from a VCR). It can also be used to combine this with still images and music. Footage from a DV camera is transferred to the computer via a FireWire cable. There are expensive video editing programs on the market; however, *iMovie* (Macintosh) and Windows *Movie Maker* (PC) are inexpensive (often free on new computers), easy-to-use consumer software programs that produce quality products.

These programs allow you to:
- transfer video to the computer
- choose the best clips
- arrange clips in any order
- add still images
- add titles and credits
- add screen transitions
- add music and sound effects
- add narration

Finished movies can be used to:
- create a videotape
- make a digital video movie for the Internet or e-mail
- store a movie on a CD or DVD

Once the video camera is connected to the computer with the FireWire cable, the computer recognizes it and loads the software needed. Onscreen controls allow you to view the video and choose the parts to use. As the video is played, it appears in the monitor area of the software. When you see a part you want to use in your "production," it is recorded in the software and stored for later use. Once these video clips are stored, you can begin the editing process. Video clips are further edited and sequenced, with some parts saved and others discarded. Once all the video clips are organized, still images, sounds, music, titles, and effects are added for the final product.

The final movie is saved in a digital video format such as Apple's *QuickTime*®, *Video for Windows*, or *MPEG*. Since digital video takes up so much space (five minutes is approximately one gigabyte), these programs compress the movie to a format that can be used in a multimedia presentation or on the Internet.

The next section provides the basic steps for producing a short movie using *iMovie*.

13.7 - Making a Movie Using *iMovie*

Getting the Video to the Computer

1. Connect the DV camcorder to a computer with a FireWire port, using a FireWire cable.
2. Turn on the camera; set to VCR/VTR/playback mode.
3. Open *iMovie*; *Create a New Project*. Give it a name.
4. The screen should read *Camera Connected* (if not, click *Camera Mode*).

5. Click on the center arrow—*Play the Camera* (be sure tape is rewound).
6. To import the entire movie, with *iMovie* detecting scene breaks (each time *Record* was pressed when the tape was shot), be sure *Start a new clip at each scene break* is specified in *Preferences: Import*.
7. To enter clips manually, click on *Import*, or press the spacebar to start and end the import of each clip.

Each clip is saved to the Clips Pane.

iMovie Work Area

1. Part of the work area is shown on the opposite page.
2. The *Pane Button* area is enlarged below.

3. Video clips are stored in the *Clips Pane* until they are ready to be used. At that time they are placed in the *Clip Viewer* (Movie Track) in the order they are to be seen. Note their length is indicated at the top; the middle one (below) is a still picture.

138

4. The *Clip Viewer* can be changed to the *Timeline Viewer* by clicking on the clock icon. In the *Timeline Viewer* each clip is represented by a horizontal bar. The length of this bar is proportional to the time the video clip occupies in the movie. (The *Timeline Viewer* adds two audio tracks and controls for other effects.)

5. When you are ready to play and edit a video clip, it is controlled with the buttons below (the *Playhead*):

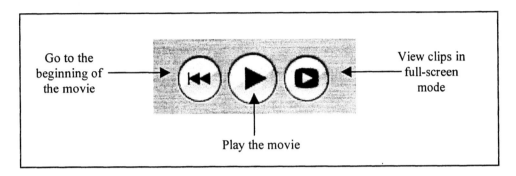

Go to the beginning of the movie

View clips in full-screen mode

Play the movie

Editing Video Clips

1. Click on a video clip to make it active.
2. Click on *Play* or the spacebar to view the clip.
3. Drag the *Playhead* (arrow under the monitor picture) to view parts of the clip. Using the right and left arrows you can view the clips one frame at a time; holding the shift key jumps ten frames at a time.
4. To crop a clip, drag the crop markers below the *Scrubber Bar* (appears below the monitor area when a video clip is selected) to indicate where the clip should begin and end. Then choose *Edit: Crop* to delete the portions not needed (areas to be cropped will turn yellow). *Edit: Cut (or Clear)* takes away the area between the arrows.
5. To view the entire movie, select *Edit: Select None*. Click on the *Play* button.
6. Select *View clips in full-screen mode* to play on the entire screen.
7. Save the movie and get ready to add titles, transitions, photos, sounds, etc.

Importing Photos

1. When a new *iMovie* is created, *iMovie* creates a folder with the name of the movie. Any other photos, sounds, etc. to be used in the movie must be placed in this folder.
2. In *iPhoto*, choose *File: Export*. Export the photos with *640 by 480* as the image size.
3. Within *iMovie*, choose *File: Import*.
4. Select the photo; *Import*.
5. Each photo is given a length of five seconds. This can be changed in the *Timeline Viewer*.

Adding Titles

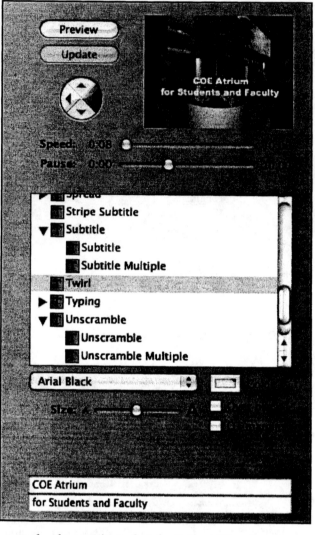

1. Click the *Titles* button to display the titles panel.
2. Enter text in the title area at the bottom of the panel.
3. Choose the style of text.
4. Text position and scrolling direction can be selected using the direction arrows.
5. Drag the title name (i.e., *Twirl* in the example) to the Timeline Viewer.
6. To add the title to the middle of the clip, split the clip first.
7. To superimpose the title over the clip, position the title to the left of the clip in the Timeline Viewer.
8. Use the slider to adjust the duration of the title.
9. To have the title on a black background instead of over the clip, click on *Over black.*

Adding Transitions

1. Click on the button for Transitions (*Tran*) in the Pane button area.
2. The transition is a motion that occurs between clips, in place of going from one clip to another without a break. They can also be put in to imply things like the passage of time, pushing to the left or right, overlapping, etc.
3. Click on the transition; view it in *Preview.*
4. To add the transition, drag it to the Timeline Viewer.
5. Drag the *Speed Slider* to change the duration.
6. To delete, click on the transition in the Timeline Viewer and press *Delete.*

Adding Effects

1. Click on the button for *Effects* in the Pane button area.
2. The effect is added to the video clip itself. Select the clip where the effect is wanted.
3. Choose an effect.
4. View it in *Preview.*
5. Use controls at the bottom of the screen to control each effect.
6. To add the effect, drag it to the Timeline Viewer.
7. Note: These can add strange effects. Use only for a purpose, and do not use too many.

Adding and Editing Sounds

If sound was a part of the video, it will be available in your movie. Sound can also be added from other sources. Using a microphone, narration can be added. To begin recording, click the red button next to the volume meter in the Audio pane. Click the red button again to stop recording. The narration is added to the first sound track.

Importing Music from an Audio CD

1. Insert the CD.
2. *iMovie* will retrieve the disc and track names.
3. Select the track you want and drag it to one of the audio tracks.

Importing Music from *iTunes*

1. Open *iTunes*.
2. Position the Playhead where you want the music to begin playing.
3. Click the *Audio* button.
4. Locate the song you want to import.
5. Click the *Place at Playhead* button.

Exporting the Movie

1. Go to *File: Share*. You will get the menu on the right.
2. To send the movie back to your digital DVD camera, click on *Videocamera*.
3. Click *Share*. The movie will be sent back to your camera.
4. For the Internet, e-mail, or to save to a CD, it is best to compress the video and save it in a *QuickTime* format.
5. Choose *QuickTime*, then the format desired.
6. Click on *Share*, then save in the desired format.

> *Note:* the instructions on the previous pages will get you started. There are many other features in iMovie. For advanced work, use the Help menu in iMovie, look for tutorials on the Web, or consult a book on iMovie.

13.8 - Activities

• Activity One •

Take a series of digital photos to use when teaching a unit of study. Possible topics could be A Day at the Zoo, Historic Philadelphia, or Trees in New Jersey. Edit and crop the photos to make them more visually appealing. Use them as the basis for a *PowerPoint* presentation.

• Activity Two •

Scan photos or diagrams from books relevant to a unit you are teaching. Use these to construct a bulletin board for your topic.

• Activity Three •

At your field experience site, take a digital photo of each student engaged in an activity. Place each picture on the top half of a sheet of paper. Have the student write about the activity in the space below.

• Activity Four •

Collaborate with your students as they take digital photos of a topic the class is studying (e.g., plants, animals, people, historical spots in the community). Put them together in a movie format that includes titles and transitions.

• Activity Five •

Take digital video of a field trip with your class. This could be a trip to a museum, a trip to the zoo, or just shots of the school. Edit the material following the instructions in this chapter. Display the video during open house.

Tool
14

Presentation Software and *PowerPoint*

PowerPoint for Teachers

14.1 - Introduction

One way to bring variation and interest into the classroom is to use a computer with presentation software to project your lesson. You can demonstrate, illustrate, and clarify information by turning your ideas and lectures into multimedia/hypermedia presentations. Students quickly tire of lecturing when it is used on a full-time basis; they will usually pay more attention, and become more involved, when ideas and concepts are projected onto a large screen. For best results, use a computer connected to a video projector. *Microsoft PowerPoint* is the most common presentation software used today.

14.2 - Presentation Software

Beginning as software to present electronic, non-linear, slide shows, presentation software now has the capability of including elements of multimedia (includes audio/video, photos, graphics, etc.) and hypermedia (non-linear; links to Web sites and other pages within the program).

Presentations can include:

- text
- graphics
- photographs
- drawings
- animations

- charts and tables
- audio
- video
- interactivity
- links to Web pages

Presentation software helps organize and enhance the delivery of content. Basic ideas and content can be turned into vibrant, exciting presentations by adding digital support. If you do not have a video projector in your classroom, most presentations can be converted to color overhead transparencies, printed on handouts, or published on a Web page. When running the presentation from a computer, it can be controlled by the presenter from the computer or a remote control or set with a timer to be used at events such as an open house.

Hypermedia authoring tools began in the late 1980s; early programs were *Linkway*® for PCs and *HyperCard*® for Macs. The next popular program for the classroom was *HyperStudio*, first issued by Roger Wagner and now available from *Knowledge Adventure*. This program, often first used in grades 4 or 5, provides tools for students to work with multimedia/hypermedia elements: cards, buttons, and backgrounds. *Kid Pix Deluxe*, which began as a drawing program for young children, now has slide shows and multimedia included. Today, the most used presentation software is *Microsoft PowerPoint*. There is also a slide show built into *AppleWorks*, and Apple now has another presentation program called *Keynote*™.

Used by teachers and students, most of these programs are similar in that they allow teachers a chance to add creativity and variety to their lessons. Students are given a chance to organize and present their thoughts, ideas, and research in presentations to their class. Presentations can include class notes, flash cards, quizzes, links to Web sites, reviews, and tutorials, to name a few.

14.3 - *Microsoft PowerPoint*

Microsoft PowerPoint, a presentation tool used by professionals in business as well as education, is available for both Macintosh and Windows platforms as a component of *Microsoft Office*. (While instructions are similar for both platforms and all versions, *Microsoft PowerPoint 2004 for Mac* is illustrated in this unit.) Often considered a vehicle to display outlines and notes, there are many other uses in the classroom. As a teacher, you can present tutorials, give quizzes, develop reviews, present games for review and reinforcement, construct flashcards, and much more. Students can produce class presentations on their research, make interactive books, do group projects, or have fun learning to make a presentation showing their drawings and class work.

PowerPoint consists of a series of slides displayed on the screen. The presentation can be self-running or controlled by the speaker. A multimedia lecture or classroom presentation can include text, clip art or digital pictures, video, and sound, along with animation. Slides can be presented in linear, as well as non-linear formats, with the order changed for different presentations as necessary. The screens (referred to as slides) are usually configured for an on-screen or large screen presentation. They can also be printed out to be used as color overhead transparencies or set up to print as presenter's outlines, audience handouts with space for notes, or handouts depicting the screens in various sizes.

A *PowerPoint Viewer* is available to show a presentation without having the program installed. This is a feature whereby the presentation can be saved as a *QuickTime* movie and viewed by anyone having the free *QuickTime* movie player installed. This can be downloaded at the Microsoft Web site. Slide shows in versions after 2000 can be saved as Web pages for viewing by others, or to use as a Web presentation.

A large selection of design templates (backgrounds) is included for presentations, or the user can begin with blank pages for custom page setups. Each template is designed with specific colors and fonts to make creating the presentation easy and visually appealing. Other templates can be found by searching various Web sites.

Included in each template is a clip art gallery and options for inserting organizational charts, tables, spreadsheet charts and graphs, columns, Web links, photos, *QuickTime* movies, and more. These can be created by the teacher or student or imported from the Web.

145

14.4 - Tips for *PowerPoint* Presentations

- Be sure text is large enough to be seen by your audience;
- Do not put too much text on each slide;
- Have contrast between the text and the background;
- Limit fonts to two per slide;
- Limit the number of fonts in the presentation;
- Restrict the number of items on each slide (text areas, clip art);
- Include only graphics that are part of the content, not just something "pretty;"
- Integrate the background with the topic;
- Do not use a complex background with a lot of text or graphics;
- Use the same background throughout, with the exception of solid color slides;
- When using large photographs or charts, use a solid color background so it does not compete with the design template;
- Include only one topic on each slide;
- Keep the same transition throughout;
- Limit sounds to those integral to the presentation;
- Remember, too much of anything distracts (sounds, animations, text, pictures);
- When presenting a lesson using *PowerPoint*, do not read the screens to your audience; use only as an outline.

Compatibility

PowerPoint is a component of *Microsoft Office*. Since there have been many versions of that over the years, there are an equal number of versions of *PowerPoint*. Although all versions are similar, the newer versions have advanced options and extended capabilities. *PowerPoint* is available for both PCs (Windows operating system) and Macintosh computers. Consequently, while *PowerPoint* is a cross-platform program (files can be used and interchanged on Macintosh and PCs), limitations do exist when moving between computers, or versions of *PowerPoint*. If working between different versions or computers, it is best to make a sample copy and try it on each computer. Animations are the least likely to transfer from one computer to another. Each version also has different backgrounds. This does not matter; once a presentation is started, the background will be saved.

Most screens are similar to those shown on the following pages. Versions prior to *2000* do not show the Outline Pane at the time screens are being constructed; however the outline can always be seen in the *Outline View*. The Formatting Palette is available in newer versions for Macintosh, and the Task Pane is available in newer versions for PC.

> *Microsoft PowerPoint 2004 for Mac is illustrated here.*

14.5 - Learning to Use *PowerPoint*

Most versions of *PowerPoint* begin with a screen similar to the screen below. This shows the workspace and the slide in a Normal view. The top of the screen has the Menu Bar and Toolbars. On the right side (not shown here), Macintosh has a Formatting Palette, while PC has a Task Pane, which can be moved to various locations on the screen. These contain visual shortcuts to items on the Menu Bar and toolbars.

The *Outline Pane* shows text that has been entered. You can also enter and organize text here that will appear on your slides. The *Notes Pane* allows you to type notes about your presentation, or organize items you want to talk about when this slide is shown. Both can be printed out in Outline or Notes views.

At the bottom of the screen are View Buttons, showing the various ways the slides can be seen.

| Normal View | Outline View | Slide View | Slide Sorter View | Slide Show |

Normal View shows the slide, the Outline Pane, and the Notes Pane.
Outline View enlarges the outline area and minimizes the slide.
Slide View shows only the slide.
Slide Sorter View shows all slides in miniature. Slides can be rearranged or deleted here.
Slide Show runs the slide show. Be sure to be on Slide One when choosing this.

Beginning a Presentation

Most new versions of *PowerPoint* open with a blank slide. The first slide to be seen is the Title Slide (right). Click, as instructed, to add text.

Design templates consist of the slide background, along with specific fonts, colors, and layout formats. They can be seen in the Formatting Palette on the Macintosh, the Task Pane on the PC, or accessed from the *Format: Slide Design* menu.

To see a sample of the design, click on the name. When using the Formatting Palette or Task Pane, the design appears on the screen. In earlier versions, a miniature slide appears. The template can be changed at any time; however some formatting might change, so try to find an appropriate template at the beginning. Some designs also have several color schemes that can be changed using the menu on the left. Each version of *PowerPoint* has different design templates. Others can be found on the Web.

Slide Layouts: new slides are accessed from the Menu Bar under *Insert: New Slide*. The layouts for the slide can be changed by choosing *Slide Layout*. A few of the choices for slide layouts appear here. Slides can also be added directly from the Formatting Palette.

The *Chart* options shown on the right exhibit data from an *Excel* worksheet.

Creating Slides

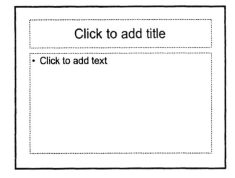

Each slide contains one or more text boxes, indicated by dotted lines. To add text, click inside the text box. Text boxes can be resized by clicking on the box, then using the new cursor and handles. They can be moved by grabbing with the hand tool and moving to a new location. Text boxes can be deleted by clicking on the box and hitting the Delete key. The slide shown here is for a bulleted list. This is also the slide to use when entering text in paragraph form. To do this, remove the bullets by clicking the *Bullets* icon in the Formatting Toolbar.

In the bulleted list, each time the Return key is "hit," another bullet appears. Design templates have varying styles of bullets. These can be changed by going to *Format: Bullets and Numbering* on the Menu Bar, or by accessing the menu from the Formatting Palette. Many different styles of bullets can be created by clicking on

Character in the *Style* menu. Bulleted items can also be indented so they appear in outline form.

Text in any text box can be changed the same as in word processing: highlight the text, then choose a new font, size, color, and/or style.

Graphics can be added to any slide. To add clip art from *PowerPoint*, click on the first icon; to add from a file, click on the second icon. The third is to insert a picture from a camera or scanner, while the forth is to insert a movie. It can also be inserted from the Menu Bar–*Insert: Picture*.

Organizational Charts (*Add Organization Chart Slide*) can be used to illustrate the administrative structure of a school, a family tree, or anything else in a hierarchical structure. This chart can be placed within a presentation or developed as a "stand alone" when a chart is needed.

When choosing the Organization Chart slide, you are then told to double click–this takes you into the Organization Chart program. When finished, go to *Organization Chart* on the Menu Bar; *Quit Organization Chart*; then *Update*. This places the chart in your presentation. It becomes a graphic with handles so it can be moved on the screen.

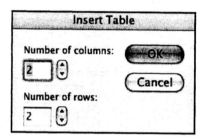

Tables (*add Table Slide*) organize a slide into boxes or cells. You can make any number of boxes for various uses by choosing the number of columns and rows. A Tables and Borders Toolbar is available to divide or merge cells, add colors and borders, and change the properties of the table.

Adding Slide Transitions

Slide Transitions are effects that occur when moving from one slide to another. When choosing *Slide Transition* in the Slide Show menu, the screen to the right appears.

From the *No Transition* pull-down menu, choose a transition to try. The *A* will change to a *B*, displaying the transition. It is best to set the speed on *Slow* and not use too many different transitions in a presentation. To apply the transition to all slides, click on *Apply to All*. To apply to only the slide you are on, choose *Apply*. These can be applied from any slide view. Sounds can also be added here.

Another option from this screen is to have the screens change after a specified number of seconds. It is not recommended to do this when giving an oral presentation, as it is difficult to determine the number of seconds needed (questions might be asked, distractions, etc). This could be used to have a presentation run continuously, such as during a school open house. To set this up, also go to: *Slide Show: Set up Show*.

Animation

Text and graphics can be animated in a presentation. Animation options are found under *Slide Show* on the Menu Bar. For example, in a bulleted list, text can enter one line at a time, giving you time to discuss it before going on to the next. On another screen you might combine graphics and text; have a graphic enter, then exit, then one section of text come in followed by another, etc. When animating more than one object on a slide, animate them in the order you want the animations to occur.

Preset animations are quick and easy to do. First click on the text box or graphic you want to animate. Then choose *Preset Animations* from *Slide Show* on the Menu Bar. Choose one of the animations. When you run the slide show, it will appear. Some include sounds, while others do not. *Laser Text* shoots the text in, while *Typewriter* types each letter. Use with caution!

Custom Animation can be used for the same purpose, but there are many more choices. Select what you want to animate, then *Add Effect*.

Movies and Sound

Movies from *QuickTime* files, or music from a file or CD, can be added to your presentation. For either, click on *Insert: Movies and Sound*.

For sound from a CD, have the CD in the computer; click on *Play CD Audio Track*. When the slide show is running, the music will begin when the slide with the music icon appears. Under *Custom Animation*, you choose the length: *Effect Options: Media Options: Stop Playing after __ slides*.

Movie from Gallery...
Movie from File...

Sound from Gallery...
Sound from File...
Play CD Audio Track...
Record Sound...

Instead of using a CD, soundtracks can be found on the Web–search for Midi files; *.MP3, .WAV*, etc. can also be used. Copy these files to the same folder as your *PowerPoint* presentation. Go to *Insert: Sound from File*; choose the sound file.

Inserting a Hyperlink (access a web site by clicking on the link)

Hyperlinks can be inserted to easily access Web sites. To do this, enter the name of the site (use the name, not the address so students can easily understand it). Highlight the site name. Go to the Menu Bar – *Insert: Hyperlink*. Enter the Web address in the *Link to* area, as shown below (copy/paste from the Web page to be sure it is correct).

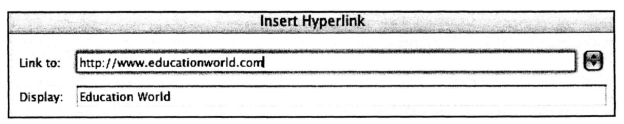

Insert Hyperlink	
Link to:	http://www.educationworld.com
Display:	Education World

Action Buttons (making *PowerPoint* non-linear)

Action buttons allow you to make *PowerPoint* non-linear. For instance, on the first screen, there can be an index. From there, you can go to any page in the presentation or you can make a quiz, going to one screen for the correct answer, another for the incorrect answer.

Custom
Home
Help
Information
Previous Slide
Next Slide
First Slide
Last Slide
Last Slide Viewed
Document
Sound
Movie

- on the slide you want to link from, go to Menu Bar: *Slide Show: Action Buttons;*
- choose where you want to go (next, previous, to another slide, etc.);
- a cross-bar cursor will appear; draw a box on your screen;
- a menu will pop up; choose the slide to link to;
- save it and try it!

Remember, in many cases you might have to put in two links (as in a quiz–one for the correct answer; another for the incorrect answer).

Saving Your Slide Show

As you progress, every slide should be saved. When saving, the above screen appears. "Presentation 1.ppt" can be replaced by any title, but be sure to keep the *.ppt* extension. Notice that *Mac 2004* is compatible with any versions back to *PowerPoint 97*.

Viewing Your Slide Show

To view your slide show go to the first slide using the scroll bar. Go to *View: Slide Show*, or use the View Buttons at the bottom left of the screen. Click on the one on the right that looks like a screen and is labeled *Slide Show*. Your first slide will now appear full-screen; use the mouse to navigate through the show. To return to *Normal View* at any time, use the ESC key.

Printing Your Slide Show

If you choose to print, *PowerPoint* will default to print the entire screen. Other options, as shown, can be printed with the correct printer settings. Each printer is different. When selecting the print menu, there will be a choice for printing options. It might indicate "Print What?," have a pull-down menu next to the word "General," or list the *PowerPoint* options. When the correct option is found, this menu will appear.

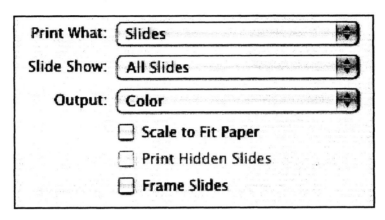

The pull-down menu from *Print What:* produces the options below.

Most of the choices are self-explanatory; *3 slides per page* provides a small space on the right for notes; *Notes* places the slide at the top with a place for notes at the bottom; *Outline* is similar to the Outline Pane, providing your students with the text of your presentation.

PowerPoint presentations can make excellent overhead transparencies. Transparency film can be purchased for your printer–be sure to purchase the correct type: laser, ink jet, etc. When making a presentation for the overhead, be sure to make light backgrounds so the light shows through, and so you do not use too much ink.

Save as a Web Page or Movie

Under *File*, you can save your presentation as a Web page or movie. *Save as Web Page* saves it in the HTML format for viewing on a Web page. If you want to save your presentation in a format that can be viewed on computers that do not have Microsoft *PowerPoint* installed, you can save it as a *PowerPoint* movie. A *PowerPoint* movie is a self-running slide show that plays in *QuickTime* Player. It uses the file extension *.mov.*

14.6 – Classroom Applications

- Class notes
- Unit review
- Project reports
- Subject tutorial
- Introduction to the school
- Open house presentations
- Year-in-review
- Personal portfolio
- Sport and club overviews
- Educational games

14.7 – Activities

• Activity One •

Develop a *PowerPoint* presentation in conjunction with a lesson plan or unit plan. (1) Make a title slide. (2) Develop at least six bulleted lists or text areas to present your information. (3) Add clip art that directly relates to the content of the slide.

• Activity Two •

Develop a *PowerPoint* presentation that is a review for a lesson you will teach. (1) Include at least five hyperlinks for information the students can study as a review. (2) As part of your slides, include factual information, not on the Web sites. (3) Make five sample test questions, with answers provided on another slide.

• Activity Three •

Develop a *PowerPoint* presentation that is an interactive test. (1) Write five questions for your students to answer. (2) For each question, create two action buttons: one will bring the student to a screen that tells them they are correct, the other to a screen that tells them they are wrong and must return to the original question.

Tool

15

Concept Maps
and
Inspiration

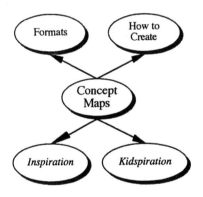

15.1 - Introduction

Concept mapping is a way to give a visual presence to ideas, concepts, facts, etc. Concept maps exist in a variety of types (highly structured to very loosely structured) and are known by a number of different names (idea maps, flowcharts, organizational charts, storyboards, hierarchical diagrams, cognitive maps, star bursts, and webs to name just a few). They are a planning/organization/presentation tool used in education, as well as in the business community and by government and industry.

Concept mapping is a technique for visualizing the relationships between different concepts, while a concept map is a diagram that shows the relationships between the concepts. These concepts, or ideas, are usually connected by arrows and sometimes linking phrases such as "leads to," "results in," "is required by," etc.

Various classroom activities can lead to concept maps.
- While brainstorming, as ideas and concepts are developed, connections can be explored between related ideas and placed in a concept map.
- Flowcharts provide step-by-step actions as a series of events is plotted out, as in a science experiment.
- Storyboards assist in laying out a project before it is created, often on the computer. This could be non-linear slides in a *PowerPoint* presentation, or pages developed for a Web site.

Concept maps can be modified and made especially appealing as a teaching aid for the intended audience if illustrations or photographs are incorporated into the presentation. Illustrations could be cut out of magazines, downloaded and printed from the Web, drawn by students, etc. This approach is often found in learning centers

A software program that is designed to assist in the creation of cognitive maps is *Inspiration*®, by Inspiration Software. This program combines the planning and the drawing aspects into one process. *Inspiration* is a tool to be used to develop ideas and organize thinking. It utilizes brainstorming, planning, organizing, outlining, diagramming, concept mapping, and webbing. Another program, *Kidspiration*®, is for grades K-5.

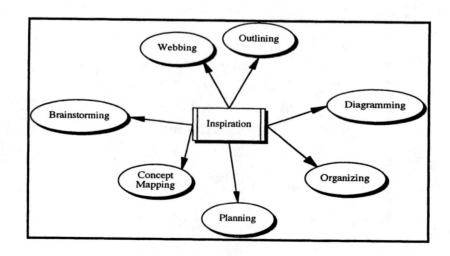

15.2 - Common Concept Map Formats

All concept maps are variations of, and can be grouped under, two basic formats: unstructured maps and structured maps.

Unstructured Concept Maps

Unstructured concept maps begin with a concept, idea, or topic and then branch out into the many related sub-topics or ideas.

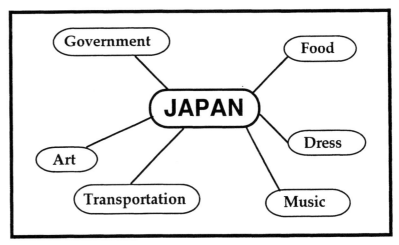

Structured Concept Maps

Structured concept maps also begin with a concept, idea, or topic and then branch out into related sub-topics or ideas. However, there is a discernible structure to the display. It exhibits "levels of consistency." All of the material identified in the map is organized into levels, and each level contains elements of equal weight, meaning, or value. Maps of this type are usually used to present or display information that is already known, or to identify voids in the organization or knowledge structure.

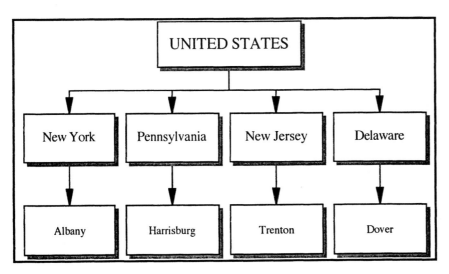

The example here is in a hierarchical structure and begins with the United States as the topic. The next level identifies the names of states. This is followed by the name of the capital of each state. The next level could be the name of the governor. This could be followed by the name of the attorney general, etc.

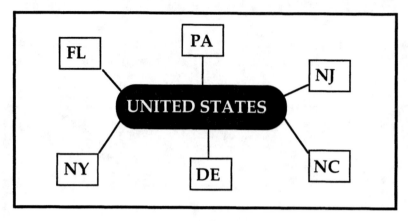

This example could also be displayed as a web or in a sunburst form. However, since it is a structured concept map, the same "levels of consistency" would be evident.

15.3 - How to Create a Concept Map

Concept maps can be created using paper and pen or a pad and a marker. These are the common tools for brainstorming or idea development work. To transform the map for educational/ display/presentation purposes, a professional and impressive looking map can be created using the draw tools of any computer program, or a program designed for this purpose. The following steps will facilitate the creation of a concept map:

1. Identify the topic or idea that will be the focal point of the concept map.
2. Select the format for the concept map that best suits the content that will be identified.
3. Using paper and pen, or a pad and marker, develop the map. (Note: It is very acceptable to cross out items at this stage of development. This is not the final product. Neatness does not count at this point.)
4. After all of the desired elements have been identified, redraw a professional looking map using the same tools or use a computer program.

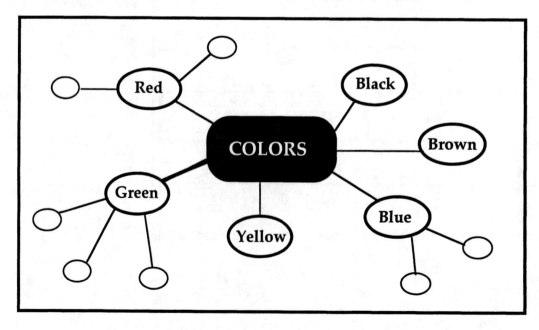

15.4 - *Inspiration*, a "Visual Learning Tool"

Inspiration can help students and teachers develop ideas and organize thinking. As a visual learning tool, it provides graphical ways of working with ideas and presenting information.

Students and teachers can:
- brainstorm
- organize information
- develop an understanding of concepts
- express and share ideas
- plan multimedia presentations (storyboard)

What is created in a diagram can then be converted to an outline. By integrating diagramming and outlining environments, *Inspiration* helps students clarify their thinking, as they better comprehend concepts and information. This also stimulates creative and critical thinking.

Inspiration encourages visual learning through the use of diagrams in the form of webs, idea maps, outlines, concept maps, and storyboards. Through these diagrams, students understand how ideas are connected and how they can be grouped together. The visual diagrams also help in the retention of information.

Webs provide a structure for ideas and show how pieces of information relate to each other. As visual maps, they help students brainstorm and organize information when writing or doing analysis. With a major topic in the center, links are made for supporting information.

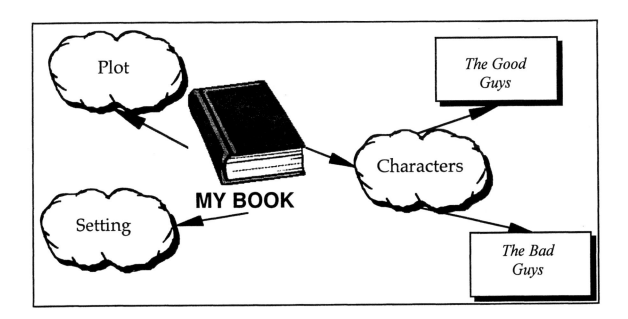

Idea maps help to generate ideas and develop thoughts. They help to clarify thinking, as students visually see connections between ideas.

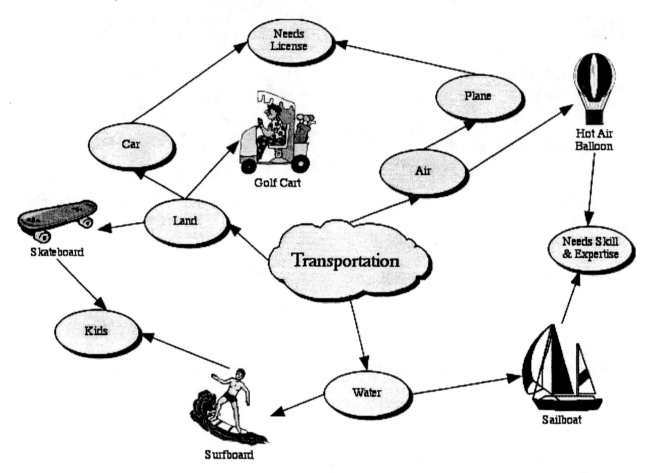

Outlines can help students organize information and present thoughts. Often used for planning a research project, information is gathered then organized in an outline form. The outline can be created and converted to a diagram, or a diagram can be converted to an outline.

Teacher Education Programs

  I. Foundations of Education

    A. Historical Base & Current State of Information

  II. Subject Area Pedagogy

    A. Content-Specific Teaching Techniques

  III. General Pedagogy

    A. Generic Teaching Methods

      1. Direct Instruction

  IV. Subject Area Content

    A. Content Structure Information

Concept maps illustrate ideas and their relationships, beginning with a general concept and working down to specifics. Links with descriptive words on them connect the key concepts.

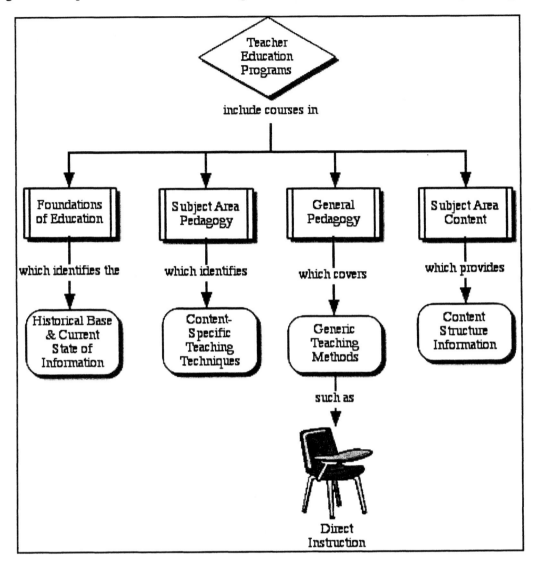

Storyboards help organize projects: what will be done first, next, and so on. Often used in multimedia projects such as a *PowerPoint* presentation, the same concept is used in developing web pages, or organizing chapters in a book.

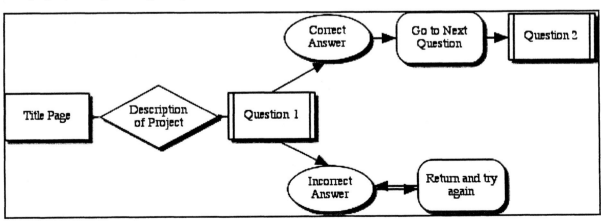

15.5 - Using *Inspiration*

Similar in concept to other drawing programs, *Inspiration* consists of tool bars and symbol palettes where choices are made. In *Inspiration 8*, there are over one million online symbols -- illustrations, photos, and animations that can be used in the diagrams. When the program opens, the *Inspiration Starter Menu* appears. Here you can create a diagram or outline, or open a file, template, or training examples, help, and more. Most users begin with the diagram icon. Beginning in the outline mode, allows the user to enter an outline that can then be converted to a diagram.

By clicking on *Diagram*, a screen appears with the "Main Idea" symbol in the center, along with several tool and menu bars.

On the top of the screen is the **Diagram Toolbar** where symbols and links are found for key tasks. The first, *Outline*, changes from Diagram to Outline View. When in Outline View, *Diagram* will appear, to change back to Diagram View. *Note* attaches a note to a symbol. *Hyperlink* allows text to be converted to a hyperlink to link to a Web page. The *Word Guide* assists in looking up definitions, synonyms, and antonyms and in learning how to pronounce words. *Transfer* allows text in *Inspiration* to be transferred to a word processor. The other Diagram Toolbar icons will be discussed in more detail on the next pages.

Adding and Linking Symbols

When the program opens, a "Main Idea" symbol appears. Additonal symbols can be placed on the screen in three ways:

1. Click on the screen and type; this creates an unconnected symbol (no links).
2. Use the *RapidFire* tool in the Diagram Toolbar. Connected or unconnected ideas can be added instantly. Using this mode, you can concentrate on adding ideas, not worrying about where to place them. To use this, click on a symbol, then the RapidFire tool. A red symbol appears. Type ideas, pressing *Return* or *Enter* after each idea. Symbols appear and can be moved and linked later.
3. Click on a symbol (get handles) to make it active; go to the *Create* tool in the Diagram Toolbar. A symbol, with a link, can be added in eight directions.

When any symbol appears, text can be added. This can be changed using the toolbar at the bottom on the screen. (One click on a symbol gives it "handles to make it active;" two clicks activates the text mode to enter or change text.)

Links (arrows) connect the symbols. If the symbols were not connected when they were placed on the screen, they can be linked with the *Link* tool in the Diagram Toolbar. Click on the Link tool, then click from one symbol to the next where links are needed.

Arranging Symbols

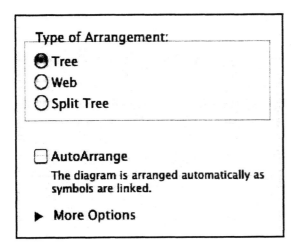

Once symbols appear on the screen, they can be arranged in various ways. *Arrange* in the Diagram Toolbar assists in changing the arrangement. Trees, Webs, and other arrangements can be chosen here.

Formatting Toolbar

Choices in the Formatting Toolbar are available to: change font, size, style of text, and text color. Also available are drawing tools, symbol color changes, and more. The "hand" moves the graphics around on the screen.

Symbol Palette

On the left of the Diagram View is the Symbol Palette, which contains libraries of symbols for the diagrams. *Inspiration 8* houses over 1,000 symbols in the libraries within *Inspiration* and also has a *Search* to find over one million symbols online.

Clicking on *Basic* provides an index of topics for the libraries. The arrows at the bottom of the screen go through the libraries. One of the libraries is show on the right.

Search searches both the online and built-in libraries.

To change an idea to a symbol, click on it to get "handles" (left, below). Choose the idea to be replaced; the idea will change to a symbol, with the text being positioned below (right, below).

Book

Links

Links can be created with the Link tool in the Diagram Toolbar. These can be edited by clicking on them (get handles). Go to *Link* in the Menu Bar to: change arrowheads, reverse direction, change angles, make curved links, hide links, and more. Go to *Effect* in the Menu Bar to change thickness, add dashes, add patterns, and change the color. Also, when clicking on the Link, a text box appears where text connections can be inserted.

Scan through the Menu Bar for more options, or go to the *Inspiration* Web site www.inspiraton.com for more hints.

15.6 - *Kidspiration*

Kidspiration, a companion program for visual learning at an earlier age, is for grades K-5. Younger students can combine pictures, text, and spoken words to represent thoughts and information. Students can categorize and group ideas, express and organize thoughts, and communicate ideas. Use of the program is similar, but with a different graphical appearance (below). The Symbol Palette (left) works the same, with the orange arrow linking to the Symbol Libraries. The icons on the Diagram Toolbar (top) are described below. The Formatting Toolbar is at the bottom. Many icons are the same as *Inspiration*, as indicated.

Go to Writing (Outline)

Add Symbol (Create)

Link Symbols (Link)

Super Grouper (adds symbols in various ways; select symbols, then add to diagram)

Clear (deletes)

Undo (undo last task)

Listen (reads words in a symbol)

Student Name (adds name to paper)

Symbol Maker (Drawing tools, more)

15.7 - Other Things to Know

- Files can be exported as *.GIF* or *.JPEG* to save the file as a graphic.
- Graphics from the Internet or other programs can be imported.
- Files can be printed; for wide documents, choose *File: Page Setup: Landscape (wide)* format.
- *Inspiration* is also available for handhelds.
- A free 30-day trial for either *Kidspiration* or *Inspiration* is available from *Inspiration's* Web site: www.inspiration.com.
- Templates, Curriculum Packets, Documentation, Examples, and Training Video are available at the Startup Menu.
- To make a symbol for text only (no symbol), click on the symbol, then the "a" in the Symbol Palette. The symbol will disappear, leaving only text. Change font size to enlarge for a title on the page.

15.8 - Activities

• Activity One •

Create a web for a book you might teach. Include a main idea, three sub-topics, and three topics under each sub-topic. Include at least three symbols from the library to enhance the diagram.

• Activity Two •

Use *Inspiration* to design a concept map for a lesson you will be teaching. The main idea should be the lesson topic. Include a minimum of 12 symbols and three graphics. Add a title for your diagram and your name (using the text icon ["a"] for both). Arrange the map in a visually appealing manner. Print out the map as a diagram and as an outline.

• Activity Three •

Create an activity requiring your students using *Kidspiration* or *Inspiration* (depending on grade level). The final product should be a diagram that includes a topic, three sub-topics, six other symbol topics, and four graphics.

Index